Contents

Contents

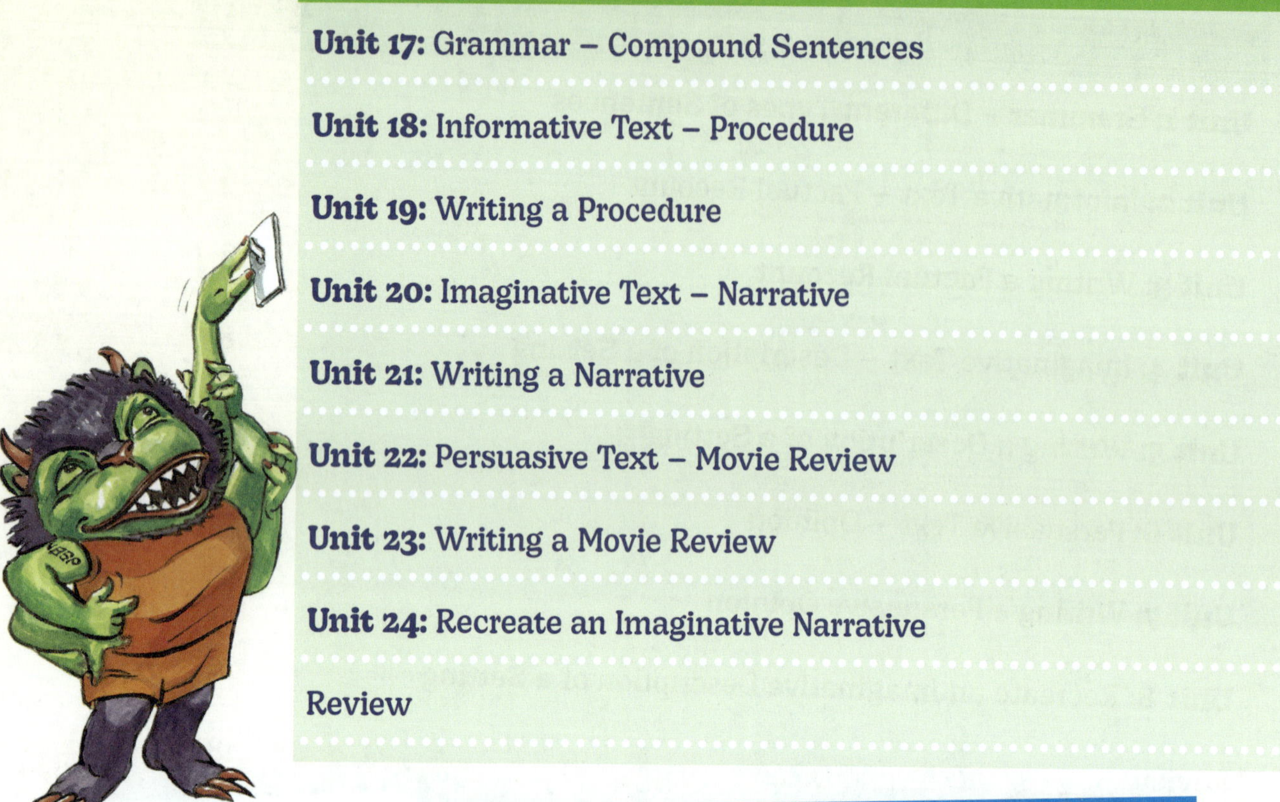

TARGETING WRITING SKILLS YR 4 © PASCAL PRESS ISBN 9781925726275

How to use this book

Targeting Writing Skills is a comprehensive program for teaching students the fundamentals of grammar and the basic structure of the three main types of texts: Informative, Imaginative and Persuasive.

This book is organised into four terms, each consisting of eight units of work followed by a review. The first unit of each term focuses on grammar, primarily on the structure of sentences. The following six units are organised in pairs, with each pair focusing on a different text type. The first unit of each pair introduces and explains the structure and features of the text type using an annotated example text. The second unit provides students with a stimulus appropriate to the text type and prompts to write their own text using the model as a guide. Each term has four units covering Informative, Imaginative and Persuasive text types.

The final unit in every term provides additional practice in writing either an imaginative or persuasive text by innovating on an existing text to change characters, setting or point of view. As these are the two main text types that students encounter in NAPLAN assessments, the additional practice helps prepare them for the tests.

A review of work that has been covered concludes the term.

While the units are organised into terms, it is not necessary to complete them sequentially. Units from any section of the book can be selected to suit students' requirements. However, it is recommended that the grammar units be completed in order as each one builds upon the previous one.

The writing topics in this book were selected for their relevance to the Australian Curriculum, including HASS, Science, General Capabilities and Cross-curriculum Priorities so that these books can be used for lessons in writing across the curriculum.

The units are presented using a gradual release of responsibility model:

1 Information is presented and explained in a detailed model.
2 Students are supported to identify features of the model.
3 Students use the model as a guide to write a text of their own about a given stimulus.

Prior to writing their own texts, students are reminded of the required structure and parts of speech that they need to incorporate. They plan, draft and receive feedback on their text before writing a revised draft. At the conclusion, they conduct a self-evaluation to determine how well they adhered to the structure and included appropriate parts of speech.

Australian Curriculum Correlations

Code	Description	Pages
English: Language		
AC9E4LA02	identify the subjective language of opinion and feeling, and the objective language of factual reporting	4–7, 12–15, 18, 19, 22–25, 30–37, 40–43, 48–51, 58–61, 66–73
AC9E4LA03	identify how texts across the curriculum have different language features and are typically organised into characteristic stages depending on purposes	4–19, 22–37, 40–55, 58–73
AC9E4LA04	identify how text connectives including temporal and conditional words, and topic word associations are used to sequence and connect ideas	4–9, 12–15, 18, 22–25, 30–35, 38–53, 56–71
AC9E4LA06	understand that complex sentences contain one independent clause and at least one dependent clause typically joined by a subordinating conjunction to create relationships, such as time and causality	20, 56, 57, 72
AC9E4LA07	investigate how quoted (direct) and reported (indirect) speech are used	26–29, 37, 44–47, 52, 53, 55
AC9E4LA12	understand that punctuation signals dialogue through quotation marks and that dialogue follows conventions for the use of capital letters, commas and boundary punctuation	26–29, 37, 44–47, 52, 53, 55
AC9E4LA08	understand how adverb groups/phrases and prepositional phrases work in different ways to provide circumstantial details about an activity	2–9, 12, 13, 16, 17, 20–23, 40–45, 48, 49, 52, 53, 58–61, 66–69
AC9E4LA09	understand past, present and future tenses and their impact on meaning in a sentence	4, 7, 8, 12, 22, 25, 30, 40, 43, 44, 47, 48, 53, 58–61, 66
AC9E4LA11	expand vocabulary by exploring a range of synonyms and antonyms, and using words encountered in a range of sources	4–7, 10, 15, 17, 24, 25, 32–37, 42, 43, 46, 47, 50, 51, 60, 61, 65, 68, 69, 71
English: Literature		
AC9E4LE02	describe the effects of text structures and language features in literary texts when responding to and sharing opinions	50, 51
AC9E4LE04	examine the use of literary devices and deliberate word play in literary texts, including poetry, to shape meaning	8–11, 16, 17, 19, 26–29, 37, 44, 62–65, 73
AC9E4LE05	create and edit literary texts by developing storylines, characters and settings	10, 11, 16, 17, 19, 26–29, 37, 46, 47, 52, 53, 55, 64, 65, 73
English: Literacy		
AC9E4LY03	identify the characteristic features used in imaginative, informative and persuasive texts to meet the purpose of the text	4–19, 22–37, 40–55, 58–73
AC9E4LY04	read different types of texts, integrating phonic, semantic and grammatical knowledge to read accurately and fluently, re-reading and self-correcting when needed	4, 8, 12, 16, 22, 26, 30, 34, 40, 44, 48, 52, 58, 62, 63, 66, 70
AC9E4LY06	plan, create, edit and publish written and multimodal imaginative, informative and persuasive texts, using visual features, relevant linked ideas, complex sentences, appropriate tense, synonyms and antonyms, correct spelling of multisyllabic words and simple punctuation	6, 7, 10, 11, 14–19, 24, 25, 28, 29, 32–37, 39, 42, 43, 46, 47, 50–55, 60, 61, 64, 65, 68–73

TARGETING WRITING SKILLS YR 4 © PASCAL PRESS ISBN 9781925726275

Australian Curriculum Correlations

Code	Description	Pages
HASS: Skills		
AC9HS4S02	locate, collect and record information and data from a range of sources, including annotated timelines and maps	6, 12, 18, 22
AC9HS4S04	analyse information and data, and identify perspectives	12, 14, 19, 30, 32, 34, 66
AC9HS4S06	propose actions or responses to an issue or challenge that consider possible effects of actions	6, 7, 14, 15, 33, 35, 68, 69
HASS: History		
AC9HS4K01	the diversity of First Nations Australians, their social organisation and their continuous connection to Country/Place	58
HASS: Geography		
AC9HS4K05	the importance of environments, including natural vegetation and water sources, to people and animals in Australia and on another continent	12, 24, 30, 58
AC9HS4K06	sustainable use and management of renewable and non-renewable resources, including the custodial responsibility First Nations Australians have for Country/Place	12, 30, 32, 33, 58, 66, 67
HASS: Civics and citizenship		
AC9HS4K07	the differences between "rules" and "laws", why laws are important and how they affect the lives of people	34, 40, 68–71, 73
AC9HS4K09	diversity of cultural, religious and/or social groups to which they and others in the community belong, and their importance to identity	70, 71
Science: Biological sciences		
AC9S4U01	explain the roles and interactions of consumers, producers and decomposers within a habitat and how food chains represent feeding relationships	3, 24, 39, 68
Science: Chemical sciences		
AC9S4U04	examine the properties of natural and made materials including fibres, metals, glass and plastics and consider how these properties influence their use	66
Science: Earth and space sciences		
AC9S4U02	identify sources of water and describe key processes in the water cycle, including movement of water through the sky, landscape and ocean; precipitation; evaporation; and condensation	4, 6, 12
Science: Physical sciences		
AC9S4U03	identify how forces can be exerted by one object on another and investigate the effect of frictional, gravitational and magnetic forces on the motion of objects	60

GRAMMAR Different types of sentences

A sentence is a group of words that makes sense on its own. It always has a verb. It usually has a subject and often has an object.

A **statement** is a sentence that gives information or an opinion. A statement begins with a capital letter and usually ends with a full stop.

Examples: *The caterpillars ate all the leaves. (information)*

The dreadful caterpillars ate all the best leaves. (opinion)

A **question** is a sentence that asks for more information. A question begins with a capital letter and ends with a question mark.

Example: *What ate the leaves on this plant?*

A **command** is a sentence that gives instructions or directions. A command begins with a capital letter and may end with a full stop or an exclamation mark. The first word is usually a verb, and the subject (you) is understood.

Examples: *Write your name at the top of the page.*

Close the door!

An **exclamation** is a sentence that expresses sudden surprise, joy or fright. An exclamation begins with a capital letter and ends with an exclamation mark.

Examples: *Wow! That's amazing! Yikes! I knew I could do it!*

Read these sentences. Write S for a statement, Q for a question, C for a command and E for an exclamation.

a Why did you bring your bike to school?
b The children play soccer at lunchtime.
c Remember to bring your homework.
d Fantastic news!
e This is my favourite book.

Write sentences about this picture. Use the prompts.

a (S) ______________________________

____

b (Q) ______________________________

____

c (C) ______________________________

____

d (E) ______________________________

____

Rewrite each sentence as a different sentence type.

a Trim the hedge with the shears.

____

b Our team won the match on the weekend.

____

c Did the police arrest the burglar?

____

d Look at the funny bird!

____

 TARGETING WRITING SKILLS YR 4 © PASCAL PRESS ISBN 9781925726275

GRAMMAR Run-on sentences

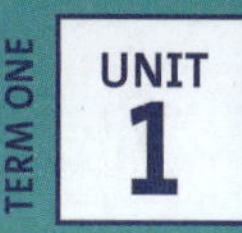

Run-on sentences occur when two or more independent clauses are not correctly combined or punctuated. They can be confusing for the reader.

Example: *My dog is smart he can do many tricks.*
To correct this run-on sentence, we add punctuation to write it as two simple sentences.
Example: *My dog is smart. He can do many tricks.*

Rewrite these run-on sentences. Use punctuation to write them correctly as two simple sentences.

a I brought my new bag to school my dad gave it to me for my birthday.

____

b The car ran out of petrol it broke down.

____

c The blue whale is the biggest mammal that ever lived it grows to 30 metres in length.

____

d There are eight planets in the solar system Earth is the third closest to the sun.

____

e Frozen water is called ice it melts when it gets hot.

____

Read this paragraph. Many of the sentences are incorrectly written as run-on sentences. Rewrite the paragraph correctly.

The Platypus

The platypus is a monotreme it is a mammal that lays eggs.

Platypuses lay their eggs in riverbank burrows the eggs hatch after about 10 days.

Platypuses live on land and in the water they have thick fur, flat paddle-like tails and webbed front feet.

A platypus uses its bill to find its way underwater and to hunt prey. When swimming, a platypus closes its nose, eyes and ears. Its bill is good for digging it also has a special ability. It can pick up electrical signals from insects, worms and frogs this is called electroreception.

Image and text from Go Facts Extreme Mammals by Ian Rohr, Blake Education.

____

____

____

____

____

____

____

INFORMATIVE TEXTS Factual recount

The purpose of a factual recount is to retell events in sequence. It often includes an evaluation of the event.

Purpose: The purpose of this recount is to retell the events of the 2003 bushfires in Canberra.

Audience: The intended audience of this recount is people who wish to have a better understanding of what happened during the bushfires.

Context: Texts like this would be found in newspapers, magazines and online.

Image and text adapted from Year 4 Comprehension and Vocabulary

Recounts often include photographs or timelines.

A title identifies the topic.

Canberra Bushfires

People in Australia live with the threat of bushfires every summer. Even major cities can be damaged by raging fires.

An orientation gives the setting and tells who, what, where and when.

Fire in the capital

It happened on 18 January 2003 in Canberra, the nation's capital. High temperatures and powerful winds combined to produce dangerous firestorms.

A series of paragraphs records the events in time order. Each paragraph has one main idea.

By the middle of the afternoon, the sky had turned red. The smoke was so thick that drivers couldn't see without their car headlights.

Everyone thought people's homes would be safe, but they weren't. The fires jumped across firebreaks. They roared into the bushy south-western suburbs. Some suburbs were evacuated. The government declared a state of emergency.

Firefighting helicopters dropped water bombs on the fires, but strong winds fanned the fires and the fire front kept growing. Flames stripped the roofs and windows from houses.

A conclusion provides a personal comment or evaluation of the events.

By the time the fires were out, four people had lost their lives. More than 350 homes had been destroyed and another 200 homes had been damaged.

Parts of Speech

Topic-related nouns and noun groups
- high temperatures
- powerful winds
- firestorms
- smoke
- firebreaks

Evaluative language
- threat
- firestorms
- evacuated
- emergency
- lost their lives
- destroyed

Time sequence words
- 18 January 2003
- by the middle of the afternoon
- by the time

Past tense
- combined
- turned
- thought
- roared
- dropped

Adverbial phrases
- in Australia
- across firebreaks
- into the bushy south-western suburbs

 TARGETING WRITING SKILLS YR 4 © PASCAL PRESS ISBN 9781925726275

Structure of a factual recount

Title

The title of a factual recount identifies the topic. Readers know that the recount will tell a sequence of events in order. In this case, it will recount the events of the Canberra bushfires in order.

Circle the title of the recount.

Orientation

The orientation gives the setting and provides details about who, what, where and when.

Highlight the orientation that provides details about who, what, where and when.

A series of paragraphs

A series of paragraphs records the events in time order. Each paragraph has one main idea.

Highlight the main idea in each paragraph. In one or two words, list the main ideas below.

a ______________________________

b ______________________________

c ______________________________

d ______________________________

Conclusion

The conclusion evaluates the events.

Underline the phrases that tell the effects of the bushfires.

Language features of a factual recount

Nouns, noun groups and appositives

Nouns are the names of things in our world such as people, places, animals and things. In a factual recount, the nouns relate to the topic. They are **topic nouns.** Topic nouns are often repeated to link the text and ensure it can be understood. Examples: *fires, firestorms*

A **noun group** is a group of words built around a noun to give more meaning to it. Examples: *raging fires, dangerous firestorms*

List nouns and noun groups that relate to fires in the text.

____

An **appositive** is a noun or phrase that is set beside another noun or pronoun to re-name it or give more information about it. It is usually separated from the noun or pronoun by a comma. Example: *in Canberra, the nation's capital*

'the nation's capital' re-names or gives more information about Canberra.

6 **Rewrite these sentences to include an appositive that re-names or gives more information about the underlined word. Remember to use commas.**

a The smoke was so thick that drivers couldn't see.

____

b The fires jumped across firebreaks.

____

c The government declared a state of emergency.

____

d Flames stripped the roofs and windows from houses.

____

Writing a factual recount

Write a factual recount about the 2022 floods in Australia.

✲ Plan

The following notes were taken from news reports about the floods that occurred in Australia in 2022.

Australian Floods 2022

- ☐ more than 20 people died
- ☐ thousands of people lost homes
- ☐ businesses ruined
- ☐ over $2 billion in damages
- ☐ one of Australia's worst-ever natural disasters
- ☐ flooding in late February, March and April 2022
- ☐ began November 2021 – wettest November on record
- ☐ wet summer – filled the catchments and saturated the ground
- ☐ February – more rain fell in short time since records began in 1800s
- ☐ wettest period and worst flooding in Australia's history – caused by combination of La Niña weather system and Southern Annular Mode
- ☐ March – flood situation was declared a national emergency
- ☐ first week in March – southern Qld and northern NSW received a year's rainfall in a week
- ☐ 7 April – Sydney got a month's rain in one day
- ☐ by end March, Sydney had already received its annual rainfall
- ☐ east coast of Australia flooding from as far north as Maryborough and as far south as Sydney

1. **Highlight the notes that give information about who, what, where and when for the orientation. Mark those notes with O.**
2. **Use a different colour to highlight the notes that could be used to provide an evaluation in the conclusion. Mark those notes with C.**
3. **Underline the words that relate to the time order in which the events occurred. Use numbers to indicate the order of events.**
4. **Write a suitable title for your recount.** ______________________________

TARGETING WRITING SKILLS YR 4 © PASCAL PRESS ISBN 9781925726275

Draft

Now you are ready to write a recount about the floods in Australia in 2022.
Remember to:

- write your title first
- write an orientation giving information about who, what, where and when
- write the sequence of events in order
- write a concluding statement that evaluates the event
- use past tense
- use nouns, noun groups and appositives
- write in sentences with capital letters and full stops.

First draft

Write a draft of your recount here.

Feedback

Ask your teacher, classmates or someone at home to suggest what you could do to improve your recount.

Revised draft

Self-evaluation

I wrote ☐ the title on the first line.
☐ an orientation.
☐ the information in the paragraphs in time sequence.
☐ in sentences with capital letters and full stops.
☐ a concluding statement with an evaluation.

I used ☐ past tense verbs.
☐ nouns, noun groups and appositives.

IMAGINATIVE TEXTS Description of a setting

The purpose of an imaginative description is to describe or give details about a character, place or object.

Purpose: The purpose of this description is to describe or give details about a setting for an imaginative story.

Audience: The intended audience of this imaginative description is children who enjoy reading adventure stories.

Context: Texts like this would be found in stories in picture books, novels and magazines. They do not usually occur on their own but form part of a longer text.

Descriptions may include illustrations.

A heading may be used to introduce the setting.

A Strange Land

An opening statement introduces the setting that will be described.

The land is tough and dry with brown grasses that feel like razors. Bark peels off trees like skin off a snake. When the wind passes through them, it feels like the land comes alive and the trees roar with strange sounds.

A series of sentences in one or more paragraphs names and describes the features of the setting.

A river winds its way through the land and empties into an enormous lake. A scrubby mountain range rises behind it.

There are thousands of flies and biting insects. At times, the noise of insects is deafening.

The bush is terrifying one minute and beautiful the next. At certain times of the day, the light makes it look like a beautiful English garden. Other times it appears to be the harshest place on Earth.

A statement concludes and evaluates the setting.

Image and text adapted from *The Unlikely Explorer* by Lisa Thompson and Andy Baker, Blake Education.

Parts of Speech

Topic-related nouns
- land
- grasses
- bark
- wind
- river
- insects

Adjectives
- tough
- dry
- brown
- strange
- enormous
- biting
- red
- black
- jagged

Similes
- feel like razors
- like skin off a snake
- like a beautiful English garden

Personification
- roar with strange sounds

Present tense
- is
- peels
- passes
- roar
- winds

TARGETING WRITING SKILLS YR 4 © PASCAL PRESS ISBN 9781925726275

Structure of an imaginative description: Setting

Heading

Although this example text has a heading, most descriptions occur as part of a longer text and will not always have a heading.

1 Circle the heading of the description.

Opening statement

The opening statement introduces the setting that will be described.

2 Highlight the opening statement that introduces the setting.

A series of sentences

A series of sentences names and describes the features.
Sentences may be arranged into paragraphs. Each sentence introduces a feature of the topic.

3 Underline the nouns that name each feature of the setting. List the features here.

Concluding statement

A statement concludes the description and may include an evaluation of the setting.

4 Highlight words and phrases in the concluding statement that provide an evaluation of the setting. List them here.

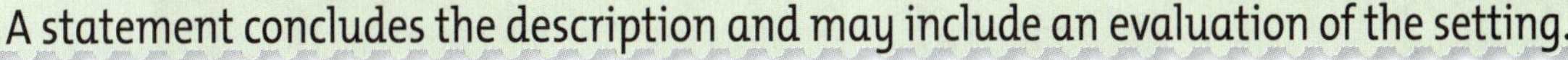

Language features of an imaginative description: Setting

Figurative language: similes, metaphors, personification

In imaginative texts, descriptions can be made interesting with figurative language and personal opinions.

A **simile** compares one thing to another using the words 'like' or 'as'.

Example: *grasses that feel like razors*

A **metaphor** compares one thing to another by saying it is the other.

Example: *grasses are razors*

Personification occurs when non-human things are given human characteristics.

Example: *trees roar with strange sounds*

5 Underline the figurative language in these sentences. Write S for simile, M for metaphor or P for personification.

- ☐ **a** The stars shone like diamonds in the night sky.
- ☐ **b** The pencil sharpener ate the tips off all the pencils.
- ☐ **c** The wind was a monster that rattled the windows and roared down the chimney.
- ☐ **d** The trees whispered secrets to each other on the breeze.
- ☐ **e** The pages were crumpled like toast that had been chewed and spat out.
- ☐ **f** A book is a door to another world.

6 Write sentences with similes, metaphors or personification to add interest to your descriptions. Write S for simile, M for metaphor or P for personification.

a house ☐ ____________________

b a bowling ball ☐ ____________________

c a video game ☐ ____________________

d Choose your own word: ☐ ____________________

IMAGINATIVE TEXTS Writing a description of a setting

Write a description of one of these story settings.

Plan

 Choose the setting you will describe. Write a heading to identify your setting.

____

 Write an opening statement to introduce your setting.

____

 List features of the setting you will describe. Use adjectives to describe them. Think about colour, shape, texture, sound, smell and movement.

____

____

____

____

 Using similes, metaphors and personification, write some phrases you could use in your description to tell what some of those features are like.

____

____

____

____

 Write a statement to conclude your description. Include an evaluation of the setting.

____

____

 TARGETING WRITING SKILLS YR 4 © PASCAL PRESS ISBN 9781925726275

Draft

Now you are ready to write a draft of your imaginative description of a setting.

Remember to:

- write your heading first
- write an opening statement to introduce your setting
- describe features of the setting using nouns and adjectives
- use figurative language like similes, metaphors and personification to add interest
- write a concluding statement that includes an evaluation of the setting
- write in sentences with capital letters and full stops.

First draft

Write a draft of your imaginative description of a setting here.

Feedback

Ask your teacher, classmates or someone at home to suggest what you could do to improve your description.

Revised draft

Self-evaluation

I wrote ☐ a heading on the first line.
☐ an opening statement to introduce my setting.
☐ a concluding statement with an evaluation of the setting.
☐ in sentences with capital letters and full stops.

I used ☐ figurative language like similes, metaphors and personification.
☐ nouns and adjectives to describe features of the setting.

PERSUASIVE TEXTS Opinion

The purpose of a persuasive text is to express opinions, either for or against a topic.

Purpose: The purpose of this persuasive text is to present a personal point of view and opinions about the need to take action on climate change now.

Audience: The intended audience of this discussion is people who need to be convinced to act now.

Context: Texts like this would be found in school newsletters, newspapers, magazines and online.

The persuasive text may be accompanied by a photograph or illustration.

A heading introduces the topic and point of view.

Stop Climate Change Now!

An opening statement attracts attention and identifies the point of view. (P)

Our climate is changing. Natural disasters like droughts, floods and fires are occurring more often and cause great destruction. The only way we can stop climate change is for everyone to help reduce greenhouse gases. Even small changes that you make can help.

A series of arguments is presented in separate paragraphs. The arguments provide evidence (E) and explain (E) reasons for holding the point of view.

Petrol-guzzling cars churn out tonnes of greenhouse gases every year. You must stop using your car every time you go out. You should walk, ride, or use buses and trains. If you must have a car, you should choose a small or electric car.

Even your home makes greenhouse gases. Reduce how much energy you use. It's easy. Use energy-efficient appliances. Turn off appliances when you are not using them. Take shorter showers.

Solar power produces zero greenhouse gases, so you should install solar panels. If everyone uses solar power, there will be fewer greenhouse gases.

A concluding statement reinforces the point of view by linking (L) back to the main argument.

We must stop climate change now. Everything we do makes a difference.

Parts of Speech

Topic-related nouns and noun-groups
- climate
- natural disasters
- climate change
- greenhouse gases
- petrol-guzzling cars

Present tense
- is
- are
- make
- reduce
- take

Modal verbs
- must
- should
- will

Emotive words
- disasters
- destruction
- petrol-guzzling
- zero

TARGETING WRITING SKILLS YR 4 © PASCAL PRESS ISBN 9781925726275

Structure of a persuasive text – Opinion

PEEL

An exposition is often written using what is known as the PEEL structure. **(P)** The heading and first statement of a persuasive text introduce the topic and point of view. In this persuasive text, the heading is 'Stop Climate Change Now!', and the first statement is 'Our climate is changing'. Readers know they will be reading about actions they can take to stop climate change.

1 Circle the heading of the persuasive text.

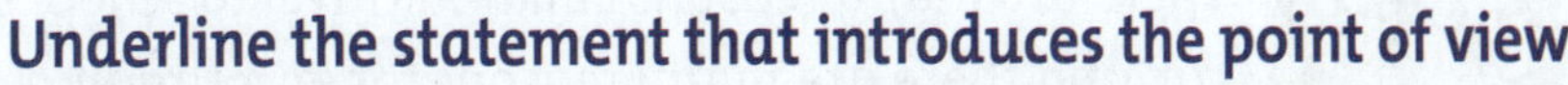

2 Underline the statement that introduces the point of view.

A series of arguments provides evidence and explains reasons for the writer's point of view. Each argument is written in a separate paragraph.
(E) The first sentence in each paragraph provides the evidence.

3 Highlight the first sentence in each paragraph that provides the evidence.

(E) The following sentences in each paragraph explain why the evidence is important.

4 Underline the sentences that explain the evidence.

(L) Each argument links back to the initial statement expressing the writer's point of view. You will see this by the repetition of the noun groups 'climate change' or 'greenhouse gases' in each paragraph. The final statement also links back to the initial statement by restating and reinforcing the writer's position.

5 Circle the final statement that reinforces the writer's position.

Arguments are often organised using the rule of 3.
The writer presents three pieces of evidence in support of the argument.

6 List the evidence.

a ______________________________

b ______________________________

c ______________________________

The writer presents two 'if ... then' statements to explain the evidence.

7 List the two 'if ... then' statements.

a ______________________________

b ______________________________

Language features of a persuasive text

Emotive words

In a persuasive text, emotive words are used to make the reader feel the same way about the topic as the writer does. They may be used alongside facts to help change the reader's opinion.

8 Read the following statements. Suggest an alternative that is better for our climate. Use emotive words to convince people to follow your suggestion.

a Air conditioners use a lot of energy and create a lot of greenhouse gases.

____

b Almost 10% of greenhouse gases come from food that is produced but not eaten.

____

c Plastic bottles can take up to 450 years to decompose in landfill.

____

PERSUASIVE TEXT Writing an opinion

Write a persuasive text to convince others to agree with your opinion about children travelling to school by car.

Fact: The use of cars contributes to greenhouse gases.
Fact: Many children travel to school by car.

There are many reasons children travel to school by car, and there are many reasons for encouraging children to choose other ways of travelling to school. Should children travel to school by car?

Plan

1. **Consider the reasons children may travel to school by car and the reasons for encouraging them to find other ways of travelling to school. List them here.**

a FOR car travel	b AGAINST car travel
______________________	______________________
______________________	______________________
______________________	______________________
______________________	______________________
______________________	______________________
______________________	______________________
______________________	______________________

2. **Choose your opinion. Should children travel to school by car?** Circle one: Yes No

3. **(P) Write your opinion as a heading:** ______________________

4. **Write an opening statement to express your point of view.**

____

5. **Choose the three most important arguments (E) to support your opinion. Write them here.**
   a ______________________
   b ______________________
   c ______________________

6. **Rewrite your most important argument as an 'if ... then' statement.**

____

7. **List emotive words you could use to convince readers to agree with your arguments.**

____
____
____

TARGETING WRITING SKILLS YR 4 © PASCAL PRESS ISBN 9781925726275

Draft

Now you are ready to write a draft of your persuasive text expressing your opinion. Remember to:

- write the title to introduce the topic
- (P) write an opening statement to identify your opinion
- (E) write short paragraphs to provide evidence for your opinion
- (E) write statements to explain why the evidence is important
- (L) restate your opinion and link your closing statement back to your opening statement
- use emotive words to influence the opinions of readers
- use capital letters at the beginning of sentences and full stops at the end.

First draft

Write a draft of your persuasive text here.

____

____

____

____

____

____

Feedback

Ask your teacher, classmates or someone at home to suggest what you could do to improve your persuasive text.

____

Revised draft

____

____

____

____

____

____

Self-evaluation

I wrote
- ☐ a title to identify the topic.
- ☐ opening statements to identify my opinion. (P)
- ☐ short paragraphs giving evidence to support my opinion. (E)
- ☐ statements explaining why my evidence was important. (E)

I restated
- ☐ my opinion and linked my closing statement back to my opening statement. (L)

I used
- ☐ emotive words.
- ☐ capital letters and full stops correctly in sentences.

RECREATING TEXTS Imaginative description of a setting

The purpose of an imaginative description is to describe or give details about a character, place or object. A description of a place is called a setting. A setting may be described in different ways by different writers depending on how the writer feels about the setting.

Purpose: In the poem *My Country* by Dorothea Mackellar, written in 1904, the writer contrasts the setting that others love (England) with the setting that she loves (Australia).

Audience: The intended audience of the poem is those who love England. The poem is written to them.

Context: Texts like this would be found in books of poetry, anthologies, newspapers and magazines.

My Country

By Dorothea Mackellar

The love of field and coppice,
Of green and shaded lanes.
Of ordered woods and gardens
Is running in your veins,
Strong love of grey-blue distance
Brown streams and soft dim skies
I know but cannot share it,
My love is otherwise.

I love a sunburnt country,
A land of sweeping plains,
Of ragged mountain ranges,
Of droughts and flooding rains.
I love her far horizons,
I love her jewel-sea,
Her beauty and her terror –
The wide brown land for me!

Although these settings are described in poetry, each verse follows the structure of a description. An opening statement introduces the setting. A series of statements describes features of the setting. A concluding statement evaluates the setting.

1 **Underline the features of each setting mentioned by the writer.**

2 **In your own words, list three features of each setting using adjectives to describe them.**

England:

a ______________________

b ______________________

c ______________________

Australia:

a ______________________

b ______________________

c ______________________

3 **Write a statement that sums up your feelings about one of the settings and explain.**

____

____

____

 TARGETING WRITING SKILLS YR 4 © PASCAL PRESS ISBN 9781925726275

Write an imaginative description of a setting

Write an imaginative description of a place, real or imaginary, where you would like to spend time. It could be an indoor or outdoor setting. Describe the features using adjectives and other figurative language to convince others how special it is to you.

Remember to:

- write your heading first
- write an opening statement to introduce the setting
- describe features of the setting using nouns and adjectives
- use figurative language like similes, metaphors and personification to add interest
- write a concluding statement that includes your evaluation of the setting
- write in sentences with capital letters and full stops.

First draft

Write a draft of your description here.

Feedback

Ask your teacher, classmates or someone at home to suggest what you could do to improve your description.

Revised draft

Self-evaluation

I wrote
- ☐ a heading on the first line.
- ☐ an opening statement to introduce my setting.
- ☐ a concluding statement with an evaluation of the setting.
- ☐ in sentences with capital letters and full stops.

I used
- ☐ nouns and adjectives to describe features of the setting.
- ☐ figurative language like similes, metaphors and personification.

REVIEW

SENTENCES – Different types of sentences

A **statement** is a sentence that gives information or an opinion.

A **question** is a sentence that asks for more information.

A **command** is a sentence that gives instructions or directions and usually begins with a verb.

An **exclamation** is a sentence that expresses sudden surprise, joy or fright.

1 Read the statements then rewrite them as a question (Q), command (C) and exclamation (E). Remember to punctuate each sentence correctly.

a The star player kicked the ball into the net.

(Q)______________________________________

(C)______________________________________

(E)______________________________________

b The children sang the school song.

(Q)______________________________________

(C)______________________________________

(E)______________________________________

RUN-ON SENTENCES

Run-on sentences occur when two or more independent clauses are not correctly combined or punctuated.

2 Read this paragraph. Many of the sentences are incorrectly written as run-on sentences. On the lines below, rewrite the paragraph using correct punctuation.

a black creature poked out from beneath the rotting logs its thin tongue searched for air the movement caught Kevin's eye was it a snake or a lizard no it was just an echidna searching for termites *Text adapted from Kevin's Echidna by Ross Pearce and David Dickson*

____

____

INFORMATIVE TEXT – Factual recount

A factual recount retells real events in sequence.

3 Use these notes to write a recount of space stations. Remember to retell the events in order and write in complete sentences.

Space Stations

- 1971 first space station – Salyut 1 – former Soviet Union
- 1971 to 1982 – seven Salyut space stations
- 1973 first United States space station – Skylab – orbited from 1973 to 1979
- 1986 Soviet Union launched Mir – in orbit until 2001
- International Space Station (ISS) launched 2000
- astronauts live and work conducting experiments on space stations
- over 200 people have made spaceflights to the ISS

____

____

____

____

IMAGINATIVE TEXT – Description of a setting

An imaginative description of a setting describes or gives details about a place, using figurative language like similes, metaphors and personification.

4 **Imagine a setting that includes the following features. Describe each of the features using adjectives and figurative language.**

a sand dunes __________

b trees __________

c water __________

d grass __________

e sky __________

5 **Write a description of the scene including the features you have described.**

PERSUASIVE TEXT – Opinion

A persuasive text expresses opinions, either for or against a topic.

One day during the holidays, you and your family go to the beach for the day. The beach is crowded with families. Everyone is having fun in the water and on the sand.

In the afternoon, when your family is leaving to go home, you notice that there is a lot of rubbish left on the beach.

What do you think about that? Is it okay for people to leave their rubbish on the beach?

6 **(P) Write your opinion about the situation as a heading.**

7 **List reasons for holding that opinion (E) and explain (E) why it is important.**

a __________

b __________

c __________

8 **Rewrite your most important argument as an 'if ... then' statement.**

9 **List emotive words you could use to influence the opinion of others.**

10 **Write a persuasive text to convince others of your opinion.**

GRAMMAR Sentences & sentence fragments

A clause is a group of words with a subject and a verb. Sentences are constructed from clauses.

A sentence is a group of words that makes sense on its own. It always has a verb. It usually has a subject and often has an object.

A simple sentence has just one independent clause and one verb.
Example: *Most books are made of paper.*

A compound sentence has two independent clauses joined by a conjunction such as *and, but, so*.
Example: *A cricket ball bounces but it needs to be hard and tough.*

A complex sentence has one independent (main) clause and one or more dependent (subordinate) clauses.
Example: *A bowling ball, which is not meant to bounce, needs to be smooth, hard and heavy.*

1 Read these sentences. In each sentence, circle the verbs, underline each clause and highlight the subject of each clause (what the clause is about).

Example:

When people make things, they choose the right materials for the job.

- **a** Synthetic materials include glass and plastic.
- **b** Materials for clothes need to be soft and lightweight.
- **c** Materials for buildings need to be hard and strong.
- **d** Plastic is waterproof, so people make water bottles with it.
- **e** Most books are made of paper because it is light and flexible.
- **f** Some books are made of plastic so babies can play with them in the bath.

Sentence fragments

If a group of words does not have a verb and does not make sense on its own, it is not a sentence. It is a **sentence fragment**. It is part of a sentence.

2 Read these groups of words. Circle the verbs, if any, in each group. Write S if the group is a sentence. Write F if the group is a fragment. In each sentence you find, add the capital letter and full stop.

Example:

[S] When people make things, they choose the right material for the job.

- [ ] **a** people use materials to make things
- [ ] **b** natural materials from the environment
- [ ] **c** scientists research how to change and mix materials
- [ ] **d** synthetic materials are made by people
- [ ] **e** materials for buildings
- [ ] **f** glass is transparent so people put it in windows
- [ ] **g** paper is a natural material made from trees
- [ ] **h** needs to be hard and tough

TARGETING WRITING SKILLS YR 4 © PASCAL PRESS ISBN 9781925726275

Sentences and sentence fragments

A **statement** gives information or expresses an opinion. It begins with a capital letter and ends with a full stop.

A **question** asks for more information. It begins with a capital letter and ends with a question mark.

A **command** gives instructions or directions. It begins with a capital letter and may end with a full stop or an exclamation mark. The first word is usually a verb, and the subject (you) is understood.

Read these sentence fragments that do not make sense on their own. Add words to turn them into complete sentences so they do make sense. Use the correct punctuation for the type of sentence you write.

Example:

The cat caught a mouse.

a into the recycling bin

____

b made of steel

____

c easily broken

____

d a type of rock

____

e synthetic material

____

f lasts a long time

____

Write some sentence fragments of your own. Ask a classmate or someone at home to turn your fragments into complete sentences. Provide feedback on their sentences, telling them two things they did well (☆) and one thing (↑) they could improve.

a Fragment: ______________________________
Sentence: ______________________________
☆ __________ ☆ __________ ↑ __________

b Fragment: ______________________________
Sentence: ______________________________
☆ __________ ☆ __________ ↑ __________

c Fragment: ______________________________
Sentence: ______________________________
☆ __________ ☆ __________ ↑ __________

d Fragment: ______________________________
Sentence: ______________________________
☆ __________ ☆ __________ ↑ __________

Sentences in this unit are adapted from Everyday Materials, a Go Facts Science book by Kara Munn

INFORMATIVE TEXTS News report

The purpose of a news report is to inform the reader of a specific event. It often includes an evaluation of the event and is very similar to a factual recount.

Purpose: The purpose of this news report is to inform readers of a new scientific discovery.

Audience: The intended audience of this news report is people who like to keep abreast of scientific discoveries.

Context: Texts like this would be found in newspapers and magazines and online.

Many news reports are accompanied by photographs.

A bold heading attracts the reader's attention.

A byline gives the name of the reporter.

An opening paragraph gives the most important information. (what, who, where, when, why).

A series of paragraphs gives more information about the events in order.

A final paragraph concludes the report and says what will happen next.

Odds and Evens are Sweet for Honeybees

By B. Sweetman

We used to think only we humans could understand odd and even numbers. Now scientists have found that honeybees can learn their odds and evens too. The scientists published their findings in the journal *Frontiers in Ecology and Evolution* in April 2022.

The scientists put the bees into two groups. They gave one group sugar water with even numbers, and a bitter liquid with odd numbers. They gave the other group sugar water with odd numbers, and the bitter liquid with even numbers. The numbers were shown with shapes like dots or triangles. They were not shown in digits.

The bees quickly learned to choose the number of shapes that would give them the sweet water. They even correctly chose numbers they had not seen before.

This discovery has helped scientists to better understand the ways brains work. Now they have many new questions to find answers to.

Parts of Speech

Topic-related nouns and noun groups
- humans
- honeybees
- scientists
- bees
- odd numbers
- sugar water

Third person
- humans
- scientists
- bees

Time sequence words
- used to think
- now
- April 2022
- quickly
- now

Past tense
- used
- published
- put
- gave
- learned

References:
Frontiers in Ecology and Evolution https://www.frontiersin.org/articles/10.3389/fevo.2022.805385/full
Reported in: The Conversation https://theconversation.com/honeybees-join-humans-as-the-only-known-animals-that-can-tell-the-difference-between-odd-and-even-numbers-181040

 TARGETING WRITING SKILLS YR 4 © PASCAL PRESS ISBN 9781925726275

Structure of a news report

Title

The headline of a news report grabs the reader's attention and identifies the topic. Readers know that this news report involves bees and odd and even numbers.

1 **Circle the headline of the news report.**

Opening paragraph

The opening paragraph gives the most important information. (what, who, where, when, why)

2 **Highlight the opening paragraph that provides details about who, what, where and when.**

Series of paragraphs

A series of paragraphs gives more information about the events in order. Each paragraph has one main idea.

3 **Underline the main idea in each paragraph. In one or two words, list the main ideas below.**

a ______________________________

b ______________________________

c ______________________________

Final paragraph

The final paragraph concludes the report explaining why it is important and saying what might happen next.

4 a Write the sentence that tells why this report is important.

____

b Underline the sentence that tells what might happen next.

Language features of a news report

Nouns and noun groups

Nouns are the names of things in our world such as people, places, animals and things.
In a news report, the nouns relate to the topic. They are **topic nouns**.
Topic nouns are often repeated to link the text and ensure it can be understood.
Example: *honeybees, bees*
A **noun group** is a group of words built around a noun to give more meaning to it.
Example: *odd numbers, sugar water*

5 **List nouns and noun groups that relate to bees in the text.**

____

Third person

News reports are usually written in the third person.
First person is the speaker (I, me, we, us).
Second person is the person being spoken to (you).
Third person is anyone or anything else (he, she, they, it).

6 **There is one sentence in the news report written in the first person.**

a Write it here.

____

b Rewrite the sentence in third person.

____

Writing a news report

Write a news report about pelicans in New South Wales.

The following notes were taken from news reports about the huge numbers of pelicans that arrived at lakes in New South Wales in early 2022.

What: over 30,000 pelicans
Where: Lake Brewster in the Lachlan Valley and Kieeta Lake in the Murrumbidgee Valley, New South Wales
When: early 2022
Why: to breed
Why: the lakes full of water and teeming with fish after a wet summer
Other facts:

- ☐ each chick eats up to 1 kilogram of food a day
- ☐ chicks and adults require 15–30 tonnes of food (1 tonne = 1000 kilograms)
- ☐ rare to have such large numbers
- ☐ last time such large numbers of pelicans arrived was after the 2016 floods
- ☐ more than twice the average number of pelicans
- ☐ not vulnerable or under threat, but numbers declining
- ☐ events like this are important for the pelican population
- ☐ drones and artificial intelligence (AI) are used to count the pelicans
- ☐ joint study by university researchers, conservationists and state officials
- ☐ pelicans are banded so researchers can find out more about them

References:
ABC News ABC Central West / Hamish Cole Posted Sun 8 May 2022
NSW Department of Planning and Environment 9 May 2022

The information about what, where, when and why for the opening paragraph has been identified for you.

1 **Read the remaining notes. Underline the word or words that tell the main idea of each.**
Example: *food, numbers, research*

2 **Think about how you can arrange the information into paragraphs. Write numbers in the boxes to show in which paragraph you will write the information.**

3 **Write a sentence to conclude the report and say what will happen next.**

____

____

TARGETING WRITING SKILLS YR 4 © PASCAL PRESS ISBN 9781925726275

Draft

Now you are ready to write a news report about the pelicans.

Remember to:

- write a bold heading to attract the reader's attention
- write your name in a byline
- write an opening paragraph to give the most important information about what, where, when and why
- write a series of paragraphs to give more information about the event
- write a final paragraph to conclude the report and say what will happen next
- use past tense
- write in sentences with capital letters and full stops.

First draft

Write a draft of your news report here.

Feedback

Ask your teacher, classmates or someone at home to suggest what you could do to improve your news report.

Revised draft

Self-evaluation

I wrote ☐ the headline on the first line.
☐ my name in a byline.
☐ an opening paragraph to give the most important information.
☐ a series of paragraphs giving more information.
☐ a final paragraph to conclude the report and say what will happen next.
☐ in sentences with capital letters and full stops.

I used ☐ past tense verbs.

IMAGINATIVE TEXTS Comic strip

The purpose of a comic strip is to tell a story using a sequence of images and limited text. Most comic strips are humorous, but some can be serious.

Purpose: The purpose of this comic strip is to tell a humorous story about things kids say.

Audience: The intended audience of this comic strip is children who enjoy humorous stories.

Context: Comic strips are often found in newspapers and magazines.

Writing Centres, Merryn Whitfield, Blake Education.

My four-year-old daughter came to me and said, "Daddy, I'm bored. Can I play outside now?"

I was a bit worried about this because we had been renovating our veranda and there were still some leftover nails and small pieces of timber lying around. But it was a lovely day for playing outside, so I agreed.

"Ok sweetie," I said. "But make sure you don't have bare feet."

Georgie looked carefully at her feet and wiggled her toes. Then she looked at me.

"But Daddy," she said. "I don't have bear feet. I have people feet."

You can see that the story has a beginning, a middle and end.

The comic strip has the same beginning, middle and end.

However, the anecdote and the comic strip tell the story in different ways.

- In the anecdote, the story is told in words. In the comic strip, the story is shown in images.
- In the anecdote, the dialogue is shown by inverted commas or speech marks. In the comic strip, the dialogue is shown in speech bubbles.
- In the anecdote, we are told what the characters are thinking. In the comic strip, thought bubbles are used to show what they are thinking.

 TARGETING WRITING SKILLS YR 4 © PASCAL PRESS ISBN 9781925726275

Structure of a comic strip

Title

Most comic strips have a title that refers to the main idea of the story.

1 **Circle the title of the comic strip.**

Beginning, middle and end

All stories have a beginning, a middle and an end.
The comic strip is a story told with a sequence of three images showing the beginning, the middle and the end of the story. It tells the same story as the anecdote.

2
- **a** Write **B** where the anecdote begins. Draw brackets [ ] around all the text in the beginning of the anecdote.
- **b** Write **M** where the middle of the anecdote begins. Draw brackets [ ] around all the text in the middle of the anecdote.
- **c** Write **E** where the end of the anecdote begins. Draw brackets [ ] around all the text in the end of the anecdote.

Language features of a comic strip

Direct speech – Speech bubbles and speech marks

Direct speech refers to the words that are spoken by one person to another.
In comic strips, the words are shown in speech bubbles. No speech marks or saying words like 'said' are used.
In text, speech marks are used to show which words are spoken by one person to another. Saying words tell us who said them.

3
- **a** In the anecdote, use one colour to highlight the words spoken by Georgie.
- **b** Use another colour to highlight the words spoken by her father.
- **c** Circle the saying words that tell you who spoke.

Thought bubbles

Thought bubbles are used to show what the characters are thinking.

4 **Underline the words in the anecdote that tell you what the father is thinking.**

5 **Underline the words in the anecdote that tell you what Georgie is thinking.**

Writing speech bubbles

Remember, speech marks and saying words are not needed in speech bubbles.

6 **Read the following sentences. Underline the direct speech. Then write the direct speech in the speech bubbles. Think about how the other character would respond. Write it in a speech or thought bubble too.**

- **a** Jack sneaked into the giant's castle. "Fe Fi Fo Fum," roared the giant.
- **b** "Can you give me a hand?" asked Sophia. "But I don't have a spare," said Alana.

7 **Write words in the speech bubbles.**

FOCUS ON IMAGINATIVE TEXTS Writing a comic strip

1 **Read this story. Highlight the title. This will be the title of your comic strip.**

A Fishy Tale

Alex had a terrible day fishing on the lake. He sat in the blazing sun all day and didn't catch even one fish.

On the way home, he stopped at the fish shop. He ordered four rainbow trout. "Pick out four big ones and throw them at me," he said to the fishmonger.

The fishmonger was confused, but he did what Alex asked. Alex caught the parcel of fish in both hands.

When Alex got home, he gave the fish to his mother.

"Did you catch them yourself?" she asked.

"I sure did," said Alex.

Targeting Homework, Year 4, Pascal Press.

2 **Circle the characters in the story. List them here:**

a ______________________________

b ______________________________

c ______________________________

3 **Use different colours to highlight the words spoken by each character.**

Beginning, middle and end

4
a Write **B** where the story begins. Draw brackets [ ] around all the text in the beginning of the story.
b Write **M** where the middle of the story begins. Draw brackets [ ] around all the text in the middle of the story.
c Write **E** where the end of the story begins. Draw brackets [ ] around all the text in the end of the story.

Plan

5
a Write a sentence to tell what you will draw in your first box, the beginning of your story.

____

b List the speaking and thinking bubbles you will need for the characters.

____

6
a Write a sentence to tell what you will draw in your second box, the middle of your story.

____

b List the speaking and thinking bubbles you will need for the characters.

____

7
a Write a sentence to tell what you will draw in your third box, the end of your story.

____

b List the speaking and thinking bubbles you will need for the characters.

____

Note: It is not necessary for the words in the speaking and thinking bubbles to exactly match the words in the story. Your illustrations do not need to be perfect. It is okay to use shapes and stick figures.

TARGETING WRITING SKILLS YR 4 © PASCAL PRESS ISBN 9781925726275

Draft

Now you are ready to write a draft of your comic strip.
Remember to:

- give your comic strip a title
- draw pictures in the boxes to show what is happening at the beginning, middle and end of your story
- add speech bubbles to show what the characters are saying
- add thought bubbles to show what the characters are thinking
- use personal pronouns when the characters are speaking about themselves
- write in sentences with capital letters and full stops, but don't use speech marks or saying words.

First draft

Feedback

Ask your teacher, classmates or someone at home to suggest what you could do to improve your comic strip.

Revised draft

Self-evaluation

I gave ☐ my comic strip a title.
I drew ☐ pictures to show what is happening at the beginning, middle and end of my story.
I wrote ☐ in sentences with capital letters and full stops.
I didn't ☐ use speech marks.
I used ☐ speech bubbles to show what the characters are saying.
☐ thought bubbles to show what the characters are thinking.
☐ personal pronouns.

PERSUASIVE TEXTS Exposition

The purpose of an exposition is to argue the case either for or against a topic.

Purpose: The purpose of this exposition is to present an argument for reducing food waste.

Audience: The intended audience of this discussion is people who need to be convinced to reduce food waste.

Context: Texts like this would be found in school newsletters, newspapers, magazines and online.

The exposition may be accompanied by a photograph or illustration.

A heading introduces the topic and point of view.

An opening statement identifies the point of view. (P)

A series of arguments is presented in separate paragraphs. They provide evidence (E) and explain (E) reasons for holding the point of view.

A concluding statement restates the point of view and links (L) back to the main argument.

Stop Wasting Food

Food wastage produces greenhouse gases which cause climate change. We need to stop wasting food now.

Millions of people do not have enough food. However, almost one third of the food produced is wasted. If we stopped wasting food, there would be enough to feed everyone. It will help save our environment too.

When food is dumped into landfill, it begins to rot. It can take months for it to decompose. Rotting food releases methane which is much stronger than carbon dioxide. If we stopped wasting food, it would be the same as taking millions of cars off the road.

It takes a lot of water and energy to produce food. When food is wasted, the water and energy used to produce it is wasted too. Throwing away one hamburger wastes as much water as having a 90-minute shower.

Most food waste occurs in our own homes. We must purchase our food wisely and stop wasting food now.

Parts of Speech

Topic-related nouns and noun-groups
- food wastage
- greenhouse gases
- climate change
- millions of people
- food

Present tense
- produces
- cause
- need
- stop
- is

Modal verbs
- need
- will
- would
- must

Emotive words
- wasting
- not enough
- save
- rot
- wisely

Reference: OzHarvest https://www.ozharvest.org/

TARGETING WRITING SKILLS YR 4 © PASCAL PRESS ISBN 9781925726275

Structure of an exposition

PEEL

An exposition is often written using what is known as the PEEL structure.

(P) The heading and first statement of an exposition introduce the topic and point of view.

In this exposition, the heading is "Stop Wasting Food" and the first statement is "Food wastage produces greenhouse gases which cause climate change." Readers know they will be reading about why it is important to stop wasting food.

1 **Circle the heading of the exposition.**

2 **Underline the statement that introduces the point of view.**

Series of arguments

A series of arguments provides evidence and explains reasons for the writer's point of view. Each argument is written in a separate paragraph.

3 **(E) The first sentence in each paragraph provides the evidence.**

Highlight the first sentence in each paragraph that provides the evidence.

4 **(E) The following sentences in each paragraph explain why the evidence is important.**

Underline the sentences that explain the evidence.

5 **(L) Each argument links back to the initial statement expressing the writer's point of view. You will see this by the repetition of words referring to food wastage. The final statement also links back to the initial statement by restating and reinforcing the writer's position.**

Circle the final statement that restates the writer's position.

6 **Arguments are often organised using the rule of 3. The writer presents three pieces of evidence in support of the argument.**

List the evidence.

a ______________________________

b ______________________________

c ______________________________

7 **The writer presents two 'if ... then' statements to explain the evidence.**

List the two 'if ... then' statements.

a ______________________________

b ______________________________

8 **Write a third 'if ... then' statement to support the third piece of evidence.**

____

Language features of an exposition

Emotive words

In an exposition, emotive words are used to make the reader feel the same way about the topic as the writer does. They may be used alongside facts to help change the reader's opinion.

9 **Read the following statements. Suggest an alternative way of saying the same thing using stronger emotive words.**

a Millions of people do not have enough food.

____

b It takes a lot of water and energy to produce food.

____

c Food can take months to decompose in landfill.

____

Writing an exposition

Write an exposition to convince others of actions they can take to avoid wasting food and why they should.

There are many ways to reduce food waste at home and school.

There are also better ways to dispose of wasted food to reduce greenhouse gases.

Plan

1 **Think about the food that is wasted at home and school. Consider reasons why the food was not eaten and why it was wasted.**

a Add other reasons to this list.

- There was too much.
- I didn't like it.
- It was past the use by date.
- ______
- ______
- ______

b Add other ways to reduce wastage to this list.

- Serve just the right amount.
- Serve food that is enjoyable.
- Use food before it reaches the use by date.
- ______
- ______
- ______

2 **Think about ways to dispose of wasted food to decrease greenhouse gases. Add others to this list.**

- Dispose of food scraps in a compost bin.
- Dispose of food scraps in a worm farm.
- ______
- ______

3 **(P) Write your point of view as a heading:** ______

4 **Write an opening statement to express your point of view:**

______

______

5 **Write the three most important arguments (E) to support your opinion.**

a ______

b ______

c ______

TARGETING WRITING SKILLS YR 4 © PASCAL PRESS ISBN 9781925726275

Draft

Now you are ready to write a draft of your exposition.

Remember to:

- write the heading to introduce the topic
- (P) write an opening statement to identify your point of view
- (E) write a short paragraph about each of your three main arguments
- (E) write reasons in support of each argument
- (L) restate your point of view and link your concluding statement back to your opening statement
- use emotive words to influence the opinions of readers
- use capital letters at the beginning of sentences and full stops at the end.

First draft

Write a draft of your exposition here.

Feedback

Ask your teacher, classmates or someone at home to suggest what you could do to improve your exposition.

Revised draft

Self-evaluation

I wrote ☐ a heading to introduce the topic.
(P) ☐ an opening statement to identify my point of view.
(E) ☐ short paragraphs giving evidence about each of my arguments.
(E) ☐ reasons to explain my arguments.

I restated (L) ☐ my point of view and linked my concluding statement back to my opening statement.
I used ☐ emotive words.
☐ capital letters and full stops correctly in sentences.

RECREATING TEXTS Exposition

The purpose of an exposition is to argue the case either for or against a topic.

Purpose: The purpose of this exposition is to present an argument for making lunchtimes at schools shorter.

Audience: The intended audience of the exposition is parents and school administrators who make the decision about the length of lunchtime.

Context: Texts like this would be found in school newsletters, newspapers and magazines.

Read this exposition written by a grumpy person who lives next door to a school. He considers their playground fun too noisy as he can't hear his favourite television program.

School Lunchtimes Should Be Shorter

School lunchtimes are too long. They should be shorter.

Children miss out on valuable learning time when they are running around in the playground. There is so much for them to learn. They cannot learn it all when they have such long lunchtimes.

Some people say they need the exercise. I think they really need to exercise their brains. If they walked to school or rode their bikes, they would get more exercise anyway. They don't need to get it at school.

If they have a big breakfast in the morning and big afternoon tea when they get home, they won't need to eat lunch at school. That's just time wasting. Many of them throw their lunch into the bin anyway.

In fact, I don't think children need lunchtimes at school at all. They need more time in the classroom, so they will learn more and be smarter.

1 a **(P)** Circle the heading of the exposition.
b **(P)** Underline the statement that introduces the point of view.

2 a **(E)** Highlight the three arguments the writer puts forward to support his point of view.
b **(E)** Underline the sentences that explain the evidence.

3 **(L)** Circle the final statement that restates and reinforces the writer's position.

4 **Write three arguments to counter the writer's point of view. Write brief notes to explain your own point of view.**

a ______________________________

____

b ______________________________

____

c ______________________________

____

TARGETING WRITING SKILLS YR 4 © PASCAL PRESS ISBN 9781925726275

Write an exposition

Write an exposition stating your point of view about the length of lunchtimes at school.

Remember to:

- write the heading to introduce the topic
- (P) write an opening statement to identify your point of view
- (E) write a short paragraph about each of your three main arguments
- (E) write reasons in support of each argument
- (L) restate your point of view and link your concluding statement back to your opening statement
- use emotive words to influence the opinions of readers
- use capital letters at the beginning of sentences and full stops at the end.

First draft

Write a draft of your exposition here.

Feedback

Ask your teacher, classmates or someone at home to suggest what you could do to improve your exposition.

Revised draft

Self-evaluation

I wrote ☐ a heading to introduce the topic.
(P) ☐ an opening statement to identify my point of view.
(E) ☐ short paragraphs giving evidence about each of my arguments.
(E) ☐ reasons to explain my arguments.

I restated (L) ☐ my point of view and linked my concluding statement back to my opening statement.
I used ☐ emotive words.
☐ capital letters and full stops correctly in sentences.

TERM 2 REVIEW

SENTENCES AND SENTENCE FRAGMENTS

A **simple sentence** has just one independent clause and one verb.
A **compound sentence** has two independent clauses joined by a conjunction such as 'and', 'but' or 'so'.
A **complex sentence** has one independent (main) clause and one or more dependent (subordinate) clauses.
A **sentence fragment** is a part of a sentence. It does not make sense on its own.

1 **Read these groups of words. Circle the verbs, if any, in each group. Write S if the group is a sentence. Write F if the group is a fragment. In each sentence you find, add the capital letter and full stop.**

- ☐ **a** at the fish shop
- ☐ **b** dumped into landfill
- ☐ **c** a good comic strip makes me laugh
- ☐ **d** food wastage contributes to climate change when rotting food makes methane
- ☐ **e** not enough playtime

2 **Read these sentence fragments. Turn them into complete sentences so they make sense. Punctuate your sentences correctly.**

a the ways brains work

____

b lakes full of water

____

c small pieces of timber

____

INFORMATIVE TEXT – News report

A news report informs readers of a specific event.

3 **Use these notes to write a news report about the discovery of a new species of millipede in Australia. Remember to give your report a heading and a byline.**

- August 2020
- Australian scientists discovered new species of millipede
- Goldfields of Western Australia
- more than 60 metres underground
- no eyes
- 1306 legs – more than any other known creature, living or extinct
- just under 10 centimetres long
- a 'true' millipede – only one with more than one thousand legs ('millipede' means 'thousand feet')

____

____

____

____

Reference: National Geographic First true millipede discovered—new species has 1,306 legs/by Jason Bittel December 17, 2021

IMAGINATIVE TEXT – Comic strip

The purpose of a comic strip is to tell a story using a sequence of images and limited text. Most comic strips are humorous, but some can be serious.

4 Write a comic strip based on this story. Think about what the characters might do, say and think. Write their words in speech bubbles and their thoughts in thought bubbles. Your illustrations do not need to be perfect. It is okay to use shapes and stick figures.

Fishing

Two fishermen met on the pier one day.
The first fisherman had a full basket of fish. The second fisherman had caught none.
"It looks like you caught a whole school of fish," said the second fisherman. "How did you do that?"
"It was easy," said the first fisherman. "I used bookworms."

PERSUASIVE TEXT – Exposition

The purpose of an exposition is to argue the case either for or against a topic.
Some people have suggested that the school day should be longer.
They say that:

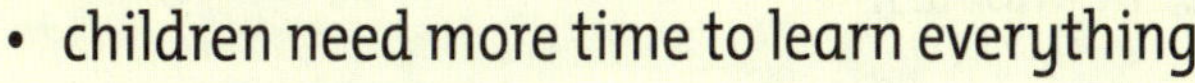

- children need more time to learn everything
- parents need more time to work without having to worry about childcare
- parents work from nine until five, children should too
- teachers' days are too short, and they should work longer.

5 (P) Write your point of view about the topic as a heading.

____

6 List reasons for holding that opinion (E) and explain (E) why it is important.

a ______________________________
b ______________________________
c ______________________________

7 Write a persuasive text to convince others of your opinion.

____
____
____
____

GRAMMAR Compound sentences

A **clause** is a group of words with a subject and a verb.

Sentences are constructed from clauses.

A compound sentence has two independent clauses joined by a conjunction: and, but, so.

Example:

Most dogs have a good sense of smell, ***and*** *they can hear well too.*

Whales live in the ocean, ***but*** *they are not fish.*

The game was cancelled, ***so*** *we went home.*

Now you will learn that compound sentences can also be joined by a conjunction: for, or, yet.

For is similar in meaning to 'because'. **Yet** is similar in meaning to 'but'.

Example:

The ball wouldn't bounce, ***for*** *it was flat.*

We can play cricket, ***or*** *we can play soccer.*

The weather forecast was for rain, ***yet*** *it stayed dry.*

We separate the two independent clauses in a compound sentence with a comma before the conjunction.

Read these compound sentences. In each sentence, circle the conjunction. Use a different colour to underline each of the independent clauses.

Example: We can ride our bikes to the beach, or we can catch the bus.

- a The car wouldn't start, for it had a flat battery.
- b We cooked the cake for the right time, yet it wasn't cooked through.
- c My big brother can play the guitar, and he can sing at the same time.
- d My mother is a teacher, but she doesn't work at my school.
- e My book was overdue at the library, so I had to return it.
- f We can go to the beach, or we can go to the movies.

Read these pairs of independent clauses (simple sentences). Form one compound sentence by using one of the conjunctions: and, but, so, for, or, yet.
Remember to use a comma before the conjunction to separate the clauses.

Example:

The ice cream was melting. I ate it quickly.

Compound sentence: The ice cream was melting, so I ate it quickly.

a I took my umbrella with me. It looked like rain.

____

b Gold is an expensive metal. It is used in a lot of jewellery.

____

c Plastic causes pollution in the ocean. We must dispose of it safely.

____

d We could watch a movie. We could go to the beach.

____

e We could watch a movie in the morning. We could go to the beach in the afternoon.

____

f The elephant is the largest land animal. It is not the largest living animal.

____

GRAMMAR More compound sentences

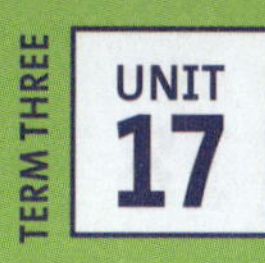

A sentence with just one independent clause is a simple sentence. It expresses one idea.
We can make sentences more interesting by combining two simple sentences or two ideas into one compound sentence.
To join sentences together, we can use the conjunctions: and, but, so, for, or, yet.

Read this text about spiders.

Spiders are arachnids. All arachnids have two body parts and eight legs. Spiders have two body parts and eight legs too. Some spiders live in webs. Some spiders live in nests. Most spiders eat insects. Some spiders use their webs to trap insects. Other spiders hunt for insects. Do not be afraid of spiders. Most spiders will not harm you. Spiders help you by eating insect pests.

The text is written using only simple sentences. It starts and stops with every sentence. We can make it flow better and be more interesting by combining pairs of independent clauses into compound sentences using a conjunction. We use a comma before the conjunction.

We can combine the following pairs of sentences to make compound sentences.

Example:

All arachnids have two body parts and eight legs, so spiders have two body parts and eight legs too. Some spiders live in webs, and some spiders live in nests. Some spiders use their webs to trap insects, but other spiders hunt for insects. Do not be afraid of spiders, for most spiders will not harm you.

Read this text about tarantulas. Find five pairs of simple sentences that can be combined to make compound sentences using the conjunctions: and, but, so, for, or, yet.

Tarantulas are the biggest spiders in the world. They are the scariest spiders in the world. They are not really dangerous to people. Tarantulas are carnivores. They eat insects and other small animals. Tarantulas are nocturnal. They hunt for food at night. Tarantulas have eight eyes. They can't see very well. Tarantulas taste with the hairs on their bodies. They smell with their feet. Many tarantulas live in burrows. Some tarantulas live in trees.

a Use different colours to circle or highlight the pairs.

b Rewrite the text on these lines so that it includes at least five compound sentences.

INFORMATIVE TEXTS Procedure

The purpose of a procedure is to give instructions, explain how to do something, tell how to get somewhere or tell the rules to be followed.

Purpose: The purpose of this procedure is to explain how to play Draw a Spider with paper, a pencil and dice.

Audience: The intended audience of this procedure is children who are learning about spiders in school or just like to have fun playing games.

Context: Texts like this would be found in children's magazines and anthologies, and online.

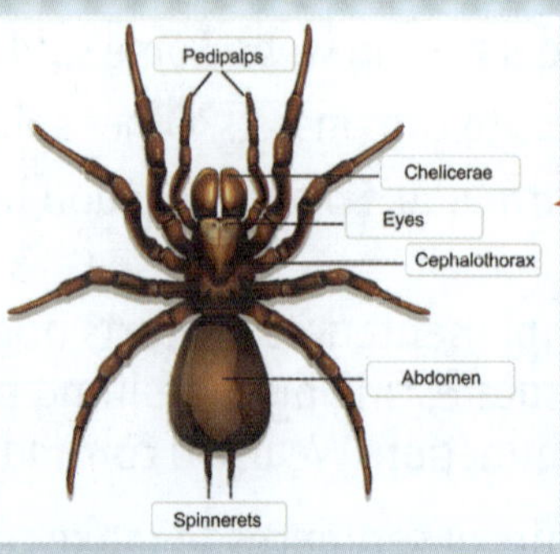

A procedure may include a photograph or illustrations to improve understanding.

A title identifies the purpose of the instructions.

Draw a Spider Dice Game

An introductory statement may also be used to explain the goal or objective.

Take turns to roll a dice and draw a spider. Draw three spiders to win. Any number can play.

Equipment

- a dice
- a pencil for each player
- a piece of paper for each player

Items required to complete the procedure are listed. Bullet points are often used.

Rules

- Draw the cephalothorax before adding other body parts.
- Draw the abdomen before adding spinnerets.
- All spiders can be in progress, but each spider requires its own rolls of the dice.

Subheadings are used for each section.

What to roll

6 = cephalothorax	3 = eyes
5 = abdomen	2 = pedipalps
4 = legs	1 = spinnerets

How to play

A series of numbered steps tells what is to be done in order.

1. Take turns to roll the dice and draw the corresponding body part.
2. Miss a turn if there is nowhere to draw the body part.
3. The first to draw three entire spiders is the winner.

Each instruction is written as a command with the verb at the beginning. The subject 'you' is said to be understood.

Parts of Speech

Topic-related nouns and noun groups
- spider
- dice
- pencil
- a piece of paper
- cephalothorax
- abdomen
- corresponding body part

Action verbs Present tense
- draw
- roll
- take
- miss

Conjunctions
- but
- and

Prepositional phrases
- to win
- before adding other body parts

 TARGETING WRITING SKILLS YR 4 © PASCAL PRESS ISBN 9781925726275

Structure of a procedure – Instructions for playing a game

Title
The title of a procedure identifies the purpose of the instructions. It tells readers what the instructions refer to.
The title of this procedure is 'Draw a Spider Dice Game'. Readers know they will be reading the instructions for playing a game.

1 Circle the title of the procedure.

Subheadings
Subheadings are used to organise the information. There are four subheadings in this procedure.

2 Highlight the subheadings.

Instructions
Instructions for playing a game may include:
- a list of equipment required for playing the game
- an explanation of rules that must be followed
- the process of playing the game in numbered steps.

The rules of this game also include a list of the numbers on a dice and the corresponding body part to be drawn when the number is rolled.

3 Underline the rules.

4 Circle the steps to be followed in playing the game.

Language features of a procedure – Instructions for playing a game

Commands and action verbs
A command is a sentence that tells you what to do. It usually begins with a verb telling you the action you need to take.
In a command, the subject is left out and is said to be understood. We know it is 'you'.
Example: *(You) Draw the cephalothorax.*

5 Reread the text. Draw a box around the action words that begin each command telling you what to do.

6 Write the action words here.

____

____

Present tense
A procedure is written in the present tense. It tells you what to do now.
A recount is written in the past tense. It tells you actions that have already been taken.

Read this recount of what I did to prepare a piece of buttered bread.

I took one slice of bread and put it on the plate.
I used the knife to scrape some butter from the container.
I used the knife to spread the butter on the bread.

7 Write the instructions I would have followed.

a List the things that I need. Remember to use bullet points.

____

____

____

b Number the actions I need to take.

____

____

____

Writing a procedure

Instructions for playing a game

Write the procedure for playing a game that you enjoy. It can be an indoor or outdoor game. It can be a pencil and paper game like the spider game, a purchased board game or a video game. You must write the instructions so that someone who hasn't played the game before will understand what to do.

In the box, draw a picture or paste a photo of the game.

Plan

1 a Write the name of the game. ______

b Write a title for your procedure using the name of the game. ______

______

2 **What is the objective or goal of the game?** ______

______

3 **List the equipment that is needed to play.**

______

______

______

4 **List the game rules.**

______

______

______

______

5 **List the actions players will perform while playing.**

______

______

______

______

6 **Use action words to write commands that tell players what to do. Number them in order**

______

______

______

______

7 **Explain how the game ends.** ______

______

TARGETING WRITING SKILLS YR 4 © PASCAL PRESS ISBN 9781925726275

Draft

Now you are ready to write a procedure explaining how to play a game.

Remember to:

- write a title to identify the name of the game
- write an introductory statement to explain the objective or goal
- use subheadings for each section
- list the items required to play the game, and remember to use bullet points
- explain the rules
- write commands to explain how to play the game, and remember to number the instructions
- use present tense
- write in sentences with capital letters and full stops.

First draft

Write a draft of your procedure here.

Feedback

Ask your teacher, classmates or someone at home to suggest what you could do to improve your procedure.

Revised draft

Self-evaluation

I wrote
- ☐ a title to identify the name of the game.
- ☐ an introductory statement to explain the objective or goal of the game.
- ☐ commands to tell players what to do.
- ☐ in present tense.
- ☐ in sentences with capital letters and full stops.

I used
- ☐ subheadings for each section.
- ☐ bullet points to list items required.

I explained ☐ the rules of the game.

I numbered ☐ the commands in order.

IMAGINATIVE TEXTS Narrative

The purpose of a narrative or story is to entertain or amuse.

Purpose: The purpose of this narrative is to entertain with a story about goats who eat anything.

Audience: The intended audience of this narrative is children.

Context: This story is part of a longer story. Stories like this would be found in anthologies and magazines for children or as a chapter of a longer story.

A story may be illustrated to aid meaning.

The title tells what the story is about.

Goats Eat Anything

The orientation gives details about who, when and where. This orientation also describes the setting.

Not so long ago, Mr and Mrs Kent lived in a cottage in the country. Along one side of the house was a cottage garden, bright with flowers. Lovely smells from the herb garden wafted everywhere and big, red strawberries waited to be picked.

Mr and Mrs Kent had to go out to work, so weeds and grass and rubbishy plants, such as fireweed, sprouted madly everywhere.

A complication or problem that affects the characters is introduced.

One day, someone gave Mr and Mrs Kent two goats.

"I hope they don't scare our grandchildren," said Mrs Kent.

"Goats eat almost anything," said Mr Kent.

"Not grandchildren I hope," said Mrs Kent, laughing.

"No," said Mr Kent. "But I hope they eat fireweed."

Mrs Kent said, "We'll soon find out."

The problem is resolved.

The next day, when the Kents got home from work, they discovered that the goats not only ate the fireweed, but they ate everything else in the garden too.

Parts of Speech

Nouns and noun groups
- cottage
- country
- cottage garden bright with flowers
- herb garden
- big, red strawberries

Proper nouns (capitals)
- Mr Kent
- Mrs Kent

Past tense
- lived
- was
- wafted
- waited
- sprouted

Time connectives
- not so long ago
- one day
- the next day
- when

Conjunctions
- not so long ago
- one day
- the next day
- when

Direct speech
- said
- inverted commas

Text adapted from The Goats, by Elizabeth Best and Janine Dawson, Blake Education.

TARGETING WRITING SKILLS YR 4 © PASCAL PRESS ISBN 9781925726275

Structure of a narrative

Title

A narrative or story has a title that provides a clue about the story. The title of this story, *Goats Eat Anything*, lets the reader know that this story will involve goats who like to eat.

1 **Circle the title of the narrative.**

Orientation

The orientation explains who the story is about and when and where it takes place.

2 **Who is the story about?** ______________________________

3 **When and where does the story take place?** ______________________________

Complication

The complication is a problem that affects one or more of the characters.

4 **What is the complication in this story?**

____

Resolution

The resolution occurs when the problem is solved.

5 **How is the problem solved in this story?**

____

Language features of a narrative

Direct speech

Direct speech is often used in narratives. It is the actual words spoken by a character. It is also called dialogue and is shown by placing **speech marks** or **inverted commas** ("__") around the words spoken.

In the story, Mrs Kent said, "I hope they don't scare our grandchildren."

We can highlight the inverted commas and underline the words that Mrs Kent said, like this:

"I hope they don't scare our grandchildren."

6 **Find those words that Mrs Kent said in the text. Highlight the inverted commas and underline the words.**

7 **Look for other inverted commas that indicate direct speech. Highlight them and underline the words that were said.**

8 **Circle all the words that tell us who said the words you have underlined.**
Example: "I hope they don't scare our grandchildren," said Mrs Kent.

Did you notice?

- Sometimes the speaker is revealed before the direct speech: Mrs Kent said, "We'll soon find out."
- Sometimes the speaker is revealed after the direct speech: "I hope they don't scare our grandchildren," said Mrs Kent.
- Sometimes the speaker is revealed in the middle of the direct speech: "No," said Mr Kent. "But I hope they eat fireweed."
- A new paragraph begins each time the speaker changes.

9 **Write P at the beginning of each paragraph that indicates a change of speaker.**

10 **Rewrite this sentence with the correct punctuation for direct speech.**
Oh no! The goats ate my strawberries, said Mrs Kent.

____

UNIT 21 FOCUS ON

IMAGINATIVE TEXTS Writing a Narrative

Write an imaginative narrative text about this illustration.

Plan

Title

What is the title of your story? Include a clue about the characters or events.

____

a Who is the story about? Remember to use capital letters for any proper nouns (names) of characters.

____

b When does the story take place?

____

c Where does the story take place?

____

a What is the problem? ______________________________

____

b What events happen to the characters and why?

____

____

____

Resolution

a How is the problem solved? ______________________________

b Who helped to solve it? ______________________________

Direct speech

Write some of the things the characters may say to each other. Remember to use inverted commas and begin a new paragraph when the speaker changes.

____

____

____

____

____

____

____

TARGETING WRITING SKILLS YR 4 © PASCAL PRESS ISBN 9781925726275

Draft

Now you are ready to write a draft of your imaginative narrative text.
Remember to:

- write the title of the story first
- begin with the orientation that tells who, what, where and when, and start it on a new line
- write the story events including a problem or complication
- use past tense
- use direct speech to report words spoken by the characters, and begin a new paragraph for each speaker
- write a resolution to show how the problem is solved
- write in sentences with capital letters at the beginning and full stops at the end.

First draft

Write a draft of your imaginative narrative here.

Feedback

Ask your teacher, classmates or someone at home to suggest what you could do to improve your imaginative narrative.

Revised draft

Self-evaluation

I wrote ☐ the title on the first line.
☐ the orientation to tell who, when and where.
☐ sentences with capital letters and full stops.
☐ story events including a problem or complication.
☐ a resolution.

I used ☐ past tense.
☐ direct speech to report the actual words spoken by characters.
☐ capital letters for the names of characters.

I started ☐ a new paragraph for each speaker.

PERSUASIVE TEXTS Movie review

The purpose of a movie review is to summarise the story and tell your thoughts or feelings about it.

Purpose: The purpose of this persuasive text is to review the movie *The Bad Guys*.

Audience: The intended audience of this movie review is others who enjoy watching movies and may be looking for the next movie to watch.

Context: Texts like this would be found in newspapers, magazines and online.

A movie review may be accompanied by a photograph of the book cover.

A heading identifies the title of the movie. Each word of the title is capitalised.

The Bad Guys

The name of the production company, the release date and the name of the director are also noted.

DreamWorks Animation, 2022
Directed by Pierre Perifel

An opening statement identifies the writer's opinion of the movie.

The Bad Guys is a very funny movie based on *The Bad Guys* books by Aaron Blabey.

One or more paragraphs tell who and what the book is about.

The bad guys are notorious villains. The gang leader is Mr Wolf. Other members are Snake, Piranha, Shark and Tarantula. The gang plans to steal a valuable award at a fancy gala, but their plan fails, and they are arrested.

To avoid jail, they ask for help to become good guys, but they are pretending. They really want another chance to steal the award. At the end, the gang decides they would rather be bad anyway.

A final judgement gives an overall opinion of the movie.

The movie is filled with twists, complications and surprises. It is both hilarious and intriguing from start to finish. Adults and children alike will enjoy *The Bad Guys*.

A concluding statement provides a rating and a recommendation.

I give *The Bad Guys* 5 out of 5 stars. I recommend it for families who like to have a laugh together.

Parts of Speech

Topic-related nouns and noun groups
- bad guys
- very funny movie
- books
- notorious villains
- valuable award
- end

Proper nouns
- The Bad Guys
- DreamWorks Animation
- Pierre Perifel
- Aaron Blabey
- Wolf
- Snake

Present tense
- is
- are
- plans
- fails
- ask

Emotive words
- very funny
- hilarious
- intriguing
- enjoy
- recommend

TARGETING WRITING SKILLS YR 4 © PASCAL PRESS ISBN 9781925726275

Structure of a movie review

Heading
The heading identifies the title of the movie to be reviewed. Each word of the title is capitalised.

a Underline the title.

b Highlight the capital letters in the title.

Heading: Movie information
The heading may include information about the company that produced the movie, the year in which the movie was released and the name of the director. This information can usually be found with an internet search.

a Underline the name of the production company.

b Underline the name of the director.

c Circle the year the movie was released.

Heading: Capital letters
Note that words in the titles of movies and the names of companies and people begin with capital letters.

a Highlight the capital letters that begin the names of the production company and the director.

b Highlight other capital letters in the text that are used at the start of proper nouns.

Opinion
The first statement presents the writer's opinion of the movie.

a Place brackets [__] around the statement that presents the writer's opinion.

b Draw two lines under the words that tell us what the writer thinks of the movie.

About the movie
One or more paragraphs tell who the movie is about and what happens in it.

Circle the paragraphs that tell what the movie is about.

Judgement
A judgement gives an overall opinion of the movie and links back to the first statement of opinion. It may give a rating and recommendation.

Highlight the judgement and recommendation that link back to the first statement.

Language features of a movie review

Emotive words
In a movie review, emotive words are used to convince the reader to feel the same way about the movie as the writer. The words will be positive if the writer enjoyed the movie or negative if they didn't.

7 **Write three statements the writer used to indicate the movie was enjoyable.**

a ______________________________

b ______________________________

c ______________________________

8 **Now rewrite those statements to show the writer did not enjoy the movie.**

a ______________________________

b ______________________________

c ______________________________

9 **Write the statement that makes you most interested in watching this movie.**

____

Writing a movie review

Write a movie review to tell others about a movie you have recently watched. Let them know what you thought of it and why. Recommend that they either watch the movie or not.

Draw a picture or paste a photo of the poster for the movie you are reviewing here.

Plan

1 **Make notes to plan your review.**

Movie title: ____________________

Production company: ____________________

Year of release: ____________________

Director: ____________________

2 **Characters:** ____________________

3 **Setting (place and time):** ____________________

4 **What was the movie mainly about? Explain in 3 or 4 sentences.**

____

____

____

5 **List emotive words to tell what you thought of the movie and why.**

____

____

6 **Write a statement to give your overall opinion of the movie.**

____

7 **Would you recommend the movie?**

____

Why?

____

8 **Who would or would not enjoy the movie?**

____

TARGETING WRITING SKILLS YR 4 © PASCAL PRESS ISBN 9781925726275

Draft

Now you are ready to write a draft of your movie review.
Remember to:

- write the title first, then include information about the production company, the year of the movie's release and the director
- write an opening statement giving your opinion of the movie
- write one or more short paragraphs to tell what the movie was mainly about
- write a final judgement using emotive words to convince the reader of your opinion
- provide a recommendation saying who might or might not enjoy the movie
- use capital letters at the beginning of sentences and full stops at the end
- use capital letters for the movie title and for proper nouns such as the names of the production company, the director and any characters.

First draft

Write a draft of your movie review here.

Feedback

Ask your teacher, classmates or someone at home to suggest what you could do to improve your movie review.

Revised draft

Self-evaluation

I wrote
- ☐ the title.
- ☐ the name of the production company, the director and the year the movie was released.
- ☐ an opening statement giving my opinion of the movie.
- ☐ one or more paragraphs telling what the movie is about.
- ☐ a final judgement sharing my opinion and recommendation.

I used
- ☐ emotive words.
- ☐ capital letters and full stops correctly in sentences.
- ☐ capitals letters for the movie's title and for proper nouns.

RECREATING TEXTS Imaginative narrative

The purpose of a narrative, or story, is to entertain or amuse.

Purpose: The purpose of this narrative is to tell a story about a boy who is dared to jump.

Audience: The intended audience of this narrative is children who like adventure stories.

Context: This story is part of a longer story. Stories like this would be found in anthologies and magazines for children or as a chapter of a longer story.

Jump!

It was the summer holidays, and the boys were playing cricket in Owen's backyard. The game was going well until Nathan hit the ball onto the roof of the garage. He climbed up to get it, but then he couldn't get down.

"Come on," said Nick. "Jump! I dare you."

Nathan wriggled to the edge of the roof and looked down. The path below where Nick and Owen were standing was made of concrete.

"Yeah, come on," said Owen. "Jump. It's not far. I did it last week, and I survived."

"Are you scared?" asked Nick.

"No," said Nathan.

Owen did a pretend yawn. He turned to Nick and said, "He's going to be up there all day. Let's go and watch TV."

"Wait," Nathan said. "Don't go. I'll jump."

Story is adapted from The Zipper by David Dickson, Blake Education.

1 Circle the title of the narrative.

2 Underline the orientation that gives details about the setting and tells who, when and where.

3 Highlight the statement where the complication or problem is introduced.

4 Choose a different coloured pencil for each character. Underline the words that were spoken and circle the words that tell you who said the words.

5 What do you think may have happened when Nathan jumped?

___

___

6 What else might have happened when Nathan jumped?

___

___

7 In this version, Nathan didn't want to jump. How might the dialogue (the words the boys said to each other) change if Nathan wanted to jump? Write some of the dialogue.

___

___

Change the point of view

In the story, Nathan doesn't want to jump. However, when he is dared to jump by Nick and Owen, he does. Change the story so that Nathan wants to jump, but Owen and Nick don't want him to.

Things to think about:

- What suggestions might Owen and Nick have for helping Nathan get down without jumping?
- What dialogue would occur between the boys?
- How would Nathan get down?
- What might happen after Nathan gets down?

Remember to:

- write the title of the story first
- begin with the orientation that tells who, when and where, and start it on a new line
- write the story events including the problem or complication
- use direct speech to report words spoken by the characters, and begin a new paragraph for each speaker
- write a resolution to the story to show how the problem is solved
- use past tense
- use capital letters for the names of characters.

First draft

Write a draft of your narrative here.

Feedback

Ask your teacher, classmates or someone at home to suggest what you could do to improve your narrative.

Revised draft

Self-evaluation

I wrote ☐ the title on the first line.
☐ the orientation to tell who, when and where.
☐ story events including a problem or complication.
☐ a resolution.

I started ☐ a new paragraph for each speaker.

I used ☐ direct speech to report the actual words spoken by characters.
☐ past tense.
☐ capital letters for the names of characters.

REVIEW

COMPOUND SENTENCES

A **compound sentence** has two independent clauses joined by a conjunction: and, but, so, for, or, yet.

1 Read these compound sentences. In each sentence, circle the conjunction. Use a different colour to underline each of the independent clauses.

- **a** The bat colony lives near us, and the bats fly over our house every evening.
- **b** Emus can't fly, but they are birds.
- **c** The man said he had a sore leg, yet he walked without a limp.
- **d** We can have pizza for dinner, or we can have fish and chips.
- **e** The children were tired when they got home, for it was a long walk from the playground.
- **f** The ground was very wet after the rain, so the soccer match was cancelled.

2 Read these pairs of independent clauses (simple sentences). Join the clauses to form one compound sentence by using one of the conjunctions: and, but, so, for, or, yet. Remember to use a comma before the conjunction to separate the independent clauses.

- **a** The lift was crowded. We waited for the next lift.
- **b** I couldn't find anything on my desk. It was very messy.
- **c** It was a very wet day. They went to the beach anyway.
- **d** The farmer went to the market. He sold his produce at a stall.
- **e** You could ride your bike to school. You could catch a bus to school.
- **f** He said he didn't like pizza. He ate it anyway.

INFORMATIVE TEXT – PROCEDURE

A procedure gives instructions or explains how to do something. These instructions tell how to play a game, but they are not written as a procedure.

It is easy to play Snap. You deal all the cards out. The first player places a card face up on the table. The next players take turns to place their card face up on top of it. If two cards are the same, players yell, "Snap!" The first one to yell, "Snap!" takes the pile of cards. Then you continue playing, taking turns to place cards and yell, "Snap!" if the cards match. You keep playing until one person has won all the cards.

3 Write a procedure to explain how to play the game.

- **a** The name of the game: ______________________________
- **b** The objective of the game: ______________________________
- **c** Items required: ______________________________
- **d** Rules of the game: ______________________________

____

- **e** How to play. Remember to write the instructions as commands. Number the instructions.

____

____

____

____

____

 TARGETING WRITING SKILLS YR 4 © PASCAL PRESS ISBN 9781925726275

IMAGINATIVE NARRATIVE

The purpose of a narrative or story is to entertain or amuse.
Dialogue, or direct speech, is used to record the words spoken by the characters.
Look at the image on the right.

Image from The Zipper by David Dickson, Blake Education.

4 **Write a title for the story.**

____

5 **Give each of the characters a name. Remember to use capital letters.**

____

6 **Write the conversation that the characters might be having. Remember to:**

- use speech marks around the words that are spoken
- use words like 'said' to show who is speaking
- start a new paragraph each time the speaker changes
- make sure every character has something to say.

____

____

____

____

____

____

____

7 **Compare two movies you have watched, one you enjoyed and one you didn't enjoy. Complete the details for each movie.**

Title: ____________	Title: ____________
Produced by: ____________	Produced by: ____________
Year: ____________	Year: ____________
Directed by: ____________	Directed by: ____________
The movie was about ____________	The movie was about ____________
I enjoyed the movie because ____________	I enjoyed the movie because ____________
Rating: ____________	Rating: ____________
Recommendation: ____________	Recommendation: ____________

GRAMMAR Complex sentences

A **clause** is a group of words with a subject and a verb.

Sentences are constructed from clauses.

A **simple sentence** is constructed from just one clause. It has one verb.

Example: *The cat climbed a tree.*

Because a simple sentence is a clause that makes sense on its own, it is called an **independent clause**.

A **compound sentence** is a sentence with two independent clauses joined by a conjunction such as: and, but, so, for, or, yet.

Example: *The cat climbed the tree, but it could not get down.*

We separate the independent clauses in a compound sentence with a comma before the conjunction.

A **complex sentence** is also constructed from two or more clauses.

In a complex sentence, there is one clause that tells the main idea. It is called the main clause or the principal clause. It makes sense on its own.

A **subordinate** or **dependent clause** gives more information about the main idea in the principal clause. Subordinate or dependent clauses do not make sense on their own. They may be linked to the principal clause by a conjunction or a relative pronoun.

Conjunctions often used to join subordinate clauses

after	as	although	and	where
because	but	if	once	whilst
so	since	then	unless	
though	therefore	until	while	
wherever	when	whenever	before	

Relative pronouns

who	whom	whose	which	that

The conjunction or relative pronoun is at the beginning of the subordinate clause. A subordinate clause can occur at the beginning, the end or in the middle of a sentence. When it is in the middle of a sentence, it is called an **embedded clause**.

Example: *The cat, that belongs to my neighbour, climbed the tree.*

In these examples of complex sentences, the main or principal clause is highlighted, the subordinate clause is underlined, and the conjunction or relative pronoun used to link the subordinate clause is circled. Notice that the subordinate clause gives more information about the main idea in the principal clause. It doesn't make sense on its own.

a The spectators, who were waiting for the match to start, were getting impatient.

b We had to get a new laptop because our old computer crashed.

c Whenever we go to the beach, we always have fish and chips for dinner.

d We always play interschool sport on Friday unless it is raining.

Read these complex sentences. Highlight the principal clause. Underline the subordinate clause. Circle the conjunction or relative pronoun used to link the clauses.

a Although Ollie ran fast, he didn't win the race.

b While we were on the bus, we saw a plane take off from the runway.

c Since it was stormy, we had my party inside.

d My favourite books are fantasy stories that have witches, wizards and magic.

e This plumber was the cheapest, therefore we gave him the job.

f If we don't act soon, the climate will continue to change.

g This is my friend whose birthday is today.

 TARGETING WRITING SKILLS YR 4 © PASCAL PRESS ISBN 9781925726275

We can change short, simple sentences into longer, complex sentences by adding subordinate clauses.

Example: The boy won the race.
Why?
The boy won the race because he trained very hard.
Which boy?
The boy who is standing on the podium won the race.
What is surprising about that?
The boy won the race although he is only ten years old.

2 **Use a conjunction or relative pronoun from the boxes to change these short, simple sentences into longer, complex sentences. Join the subordinate clauses at the beginning, the end or in the middle of some sentences.**

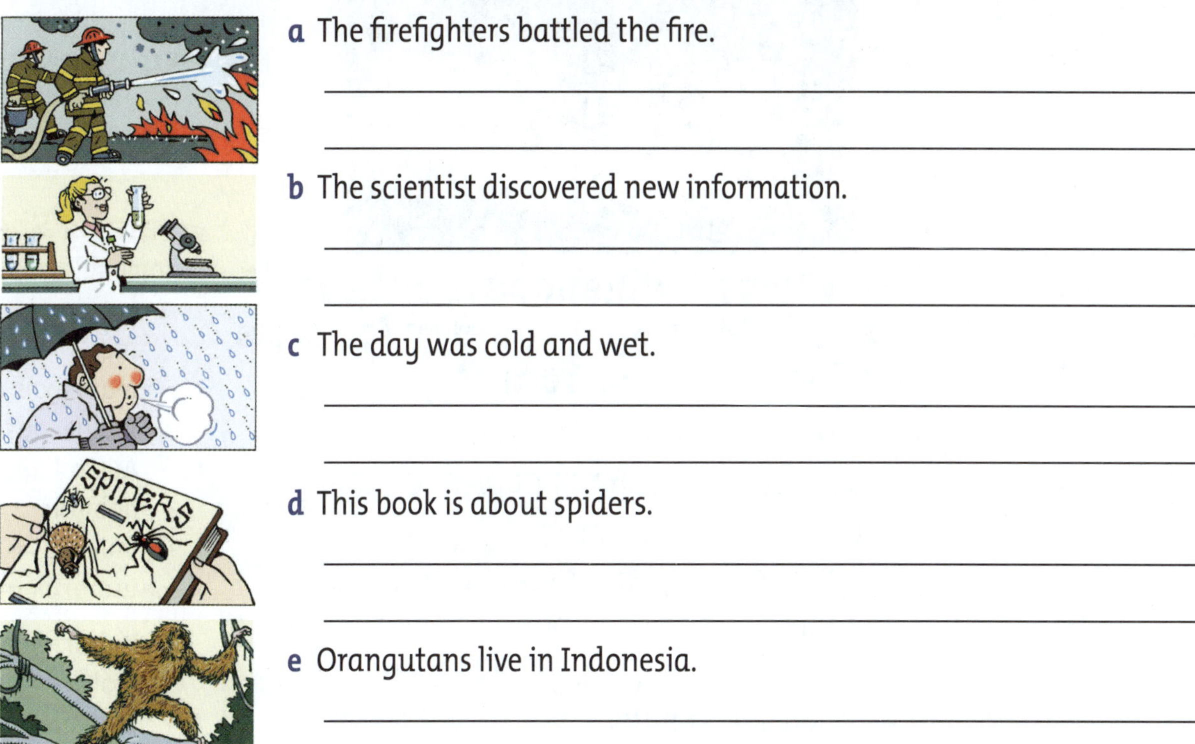

a The firefighters battled the fire.

____

____

b The scientist discovered new information.

____

____

c The day was cold and wet.

____

____

d This book is about spiders.

____

____

e Orangutans live in Indonesia.

____

____

3 **Read the following text. Put brackets (__) around the complex sentences. Highlight the principal clauses. Underline the subordinate clauses. Circle the conjunction or relative pronoun that links the clauses.**
Hint: The number of verbs in each sentence tells you the number of clauses.

Our Summer Picnic

One Sunday in summer, our family decided to go for a picnic in the mountains. After we stopped for morning tea at Grandma's house, we packed the picnic baskets into the car. We drove to a place in the mountains that is called Swanfels. The picnic ground was once part of the Swanfels School, which was closed in 1986. When we arrived at the picnic grounds, I helped my cousins with the picnic baskets. After we found a chair for Grandma, we played on the playground equipment. We had fun on the swings, monkey bars and slippery slide. Then we went for a walk. We walked along a track until we came to an old wooden bridge. When we arrived back at the picnic area, we were all very thirsty and hungry. Lunch was the best picnic that we ever had.

Text adapted from Our Summer Picnic, p 93 of Targeting Grammar 4 by Del Merrick

INFORMATIVE TEXTS Explanation

The purpose of an explanation is to explain how things happen or why things are.

Purpose: The purpose of this explanation is to explain how Indigenous Australian peoples have managed Country for tens of thousands of years.

Audience: The intended audience of this explanation is children who are learning about the long and continuous connection of Indigenous Australian peoples to Country and the effect of natural processes and human activity on Earth's surface over time.

Context: Texts like this would be found in history and science books, magazines and online.

Explanations often include photographs or diagrams.

A title is often in the form of a question. It identifies the topic.

How Have Indigenous Australian Peoples Managed Country for Tens of Thousands of Years?

A general statement introduces the topic.

Fire was one of the main tools used by Indigenous Australian peoples to manage Country.

They used fire to create habitats to attract animals to an area. When fires were burning, the animals could not get away and they were easier to hunt.

Indigenous Australian peoples knew the best times for lighting fires and made sure that only the underbrush burned. This prevented the large destructive bushfires we often see today.

A series of paragraphs shows the cause-and-effect relationships. Each paragraph explains one main idea.

The fires also helped useful plants to grow and stopped the spread of plants that weren't useful.

Fire wasn't the only tool used. Some Indigenous Australian peoples cleared land to plant crops. Others built farms for eels and traps for fish in rivers. Most changed their diet from season to season to give plants and animals time to regrow.

A concluding statement ensures the explanation is complete.

Managing Country meant that they could live sustainably for tens of thousands of years.

Parts of Speech

Topic-related nouns and noun groups
- fire
- main tools
- Indigenous Australian peoples
- habitats
- animals
- useful plants

Technical language
- tools
- manage
- habitats
- underbrush
- destructive
- sustainably

Action verbs
- used
- manage
- attract
- prevented
- cleared

Prepositional phrases
- for lighting fires
- to plant crops
- for fish
- in rivers

Text adapted from Reshaping Environments, by Nicholas Brasch

Structure of an explanation

Title

The title of an explanation identifies the topic. It is often in the form of a question. Readers know that the explanation will explain or give an answer to the question. In this case, it will explain how Indigenous Australian peoples have managed Country for tens of thousands of years.

1 **Circle the title of the explanation.**

Introductory statement

The general statement introduces the topic.

2 **Highlight the statement that introduces the topic.**

A series of paragraphs explains the causes and effects

Each paragraph has one main idea. Three paragraphs explain the benefits or effects of Indigenous Australian peoples' use of fire.

3 **Highlight the three benefits of using fire to manage Country. Write them on these lines.**

a ______________________________

b ______________________________

c ______________________________

Concluding statement

A concluding statement sums up the explanation.

4 **Write the cause and effect summed up in the concluding statement.**

a Cause: ______________________________

b Effect: ______________________________

Language features of an explanation

Action verbs and past tense

In an explanation, action verbs are used to explain what happens or happened. Explanations are often written in the present tense. Many of the practices described are still being used by Indigenous Australian peoples living a traditional life, but because this explanation tells how fire has been used over thousands of years, the past tense is used.

5 **Complete this table by writing the present tense form of the past tense verbs.**

Present	Past	Present	Past
a	was	f	prevented
b	used	g	helped
c	were	h	cleared
d	knew	i	built
e	made	j	changed

6 **These sentences are written in the past tense. Circle the verbs. Rewrite the sentences in present tense.**

a Fire was one of the main tools that Indigenous Australian peoples used to manage Country.

____

b Some Indigenous Australian peoples cleared land to plant crops.

____

INFORMATIVE TEXTS Writing an explanation

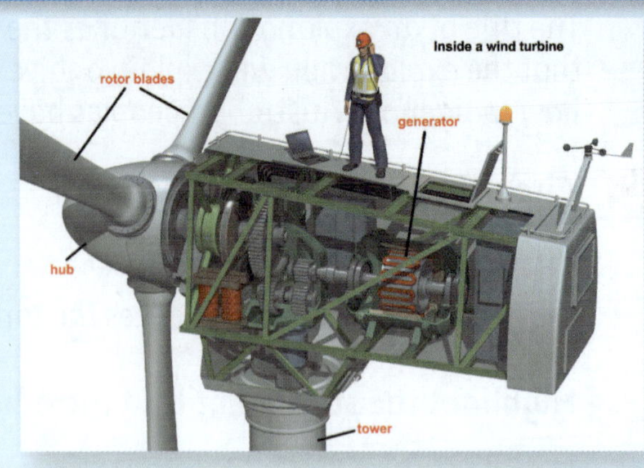

Use this diagram and these notes to write an explanation of how a wind turbine works.

- uses force of wind to produce energy
- uses no fuel, emits no pollution
- tower up to 30 metres tall
- wind blows (kinetic energy) → blades turn (mechanical energy) → rotor turns the main shaft → turns the generator → converts mechanical energy into electrical energy
- wind does not blow all the time → need other sources of energy too → unless can be stored
- best places on top of hill or near coast where windy

Plan

1. **Write a title for your explanation as a question.**

___

2. **Write a general statement to introduce your topic.**

___

3. **Write the process of turning wind into electrical energy in simple sentences and as a series of steps.**

a ___
b ___
c ___
d ___
e ___

4. **Combine pairs of sentences to show how one step causes the next step to occur.**

a ___
___
b ___
___
c ___
___

5. **The notes list a limitation of wind turbines and a recommendation. Write a concluding statement to sum up your explanation.**

___
___
___
___

6. **List any technical words that may need to be explained to your readers. Write an explanation for the words.**

a ___
b ___
c ___

7. **List action verbs you will use to explain how wind turbines work.**

___

 TARGETING WRITING SKILLS YR 4 © PASCAL PRESS ISBN 9781925726275

✲ Draft

Now you are ready to write an explanation of how wind turbines work.

Remember to:

- write your title first. It is usually written as a question.
- write a general statement to introduce your topic
- write each step in its own paragraph with supporting information
- ensure the paragraphs follow each other logically showing cause and effect
- write a concluding statement to ensure the explanation is complete
- use present tense
- write a final statement to conclude the explanation
- write in sentences with capital letters and full stops.

✲ First draft

Write a draft of your explanation here.

✲ Feedback

Ask your teacher, classmates or someone at home to suggest what you could do to improve your explanation.

✲ Revised draft

✲ Self-evaluation ✲

I wrote
- ☐ the title as a question on the first line.
- ☐ a general statement to introduce the topic.
- ☐ each step in its own paragraph with supporting information.
- ☐ a final statement to conclude the explanation.
- ☐ in present tense.
- ☐ in sentences with capital letters and full stops.

I ensured
- ☐ the paragraphs followed logically and showed cause and effect.

FOCUS ON IMAGINATIVE TEXTS Poetry

The purpose of poetry is to help us understand and appreciate the world around us.

Purpose: The purpose of this poem is to entertain and amuse with a different way of looking at nature.

Audience: The intended audience of this narrative is children.

Context: This poem was written in 1921 and was included in an anthology called *A Book for Kids* by C.J. Dennis. Poems like this are often included in other anthologies and magazines for children.

A poem may be illustrated to aid meaning.

The Triantiwontigongolope

by C. J. Dennis

There's a very funny insect that you do not often spy,
And it isn't quite a spider, and it isn't quite a fly;
It is something like a beetle, and a little like a bee,
But nothing like a woolly grub that climbs upon a tree.
Its name is quite a hard one, but you'll learn it soon, I hope.
So try:
Tri-
Tri-anti-wonti-
Triantiwontigongolope.

But of course you haven't seen it; and I truthfully confess
That I haven't seen it either, and I don't know its address.
For there isn't such an insect, though there really might have been
If the trees and grass were purple, and the sky was bottle green.
It's just a little joke of mine, which you'll forgive, I hope.
Oh, try!
Tri-
Tri-anti-wonti-
Triantiwontigongolope.

Language features of poetry

Rhyming words
- spy/fly
- bee/tree
- hope/triantiwonti-gongolope
- try/tri

Assonance (repeated vowel sounds)
- quite/spider/fly
- beetle/bee

Consonance (repeated consonant sounds)
- beetle/bee
- little/like
- trees/grass/sky
- purple/bottle

Similes
- something like a beetle
- a little like a bee

Repetition
- something like/ a little like/nothing like

Refrain
- So try:
  Tri-
  Tri-anti-wonti-
  Triantiwontigongo-lope

Poems:
- do not usually have sentences that follow the normal structure, beginning with a capital letter and ending with a full stop, like other texts do
- are usually written in verse, which means they follow a set rhythm and often include rhyme
- are usually arranged in stanzas, or groups of lines, that begin with a capital letter and end with a full stop. Each line of the stanza also begins with a capital letter whether it is a new sentence or not.

Extract from The Triantiwontigongolope by C.J. Dennis

TARGETING WRITING SKILLS YR 4 © PASCAL PRESS ISBN 9781925726275

Structure of a poem

Title
A poem usually has a title that tells you what the poem is about.

1 Circle the title of the poem.

Verse
Poems are often written in verse. They usually have a rhythm that is different from normal written text or speech. They often rhyme. The rhyming words occur at the ends of lines.

2 Read the poem. Use different colours to circle the pairs of words that rhyme.

Stanzas
Stanzas are a group of lines that begin with a capital letter and end with a full stop.
Each line in a stanza begins with a capital letter, whether it begins a new sentence or not.

3 Underline the capital letter at the beginning of each line.

Refrain
Poems often have a refrain, a group of words or lines, that is repeated within or at the end of each stanza.

4 Highlight the refrain in each stanza.

Language features of a poem

The humorous poem *The Triantiwontigongolope* was written as a joke to entertain. The poet tells us this at the end of the poem. The example on the previous page includes the first and the last stanzas. There are another two stanzas in the original poem.
The word *triantiwontigongolope* includes many features of poetry, especially humorous poetry.
neologism – a nonsense or invented word
assonance – repetition of vowel sounds (i as in anti and wonti; o as in go and lope)
consonance – repetition of consonant sounds (t as in tri, anti, wonti; g as in gongo)
These features are also used in other stanzas of the poem.

5 Read these second and third verses of the original poem out loud.
(Note: the refrain is omitted to save space.)

It lives on weeds and wattle-gum, and has a funny face;
Its appetite is hearty, and its manners a disgrace.
When first you come upon it, it will give you quite a scare,
But when you look for it again, you find it isn't there.
And unless you call it softly it will stay away and mope.

It trembles if you tickle it or tread upon its toes;
It is not an early riser, but it has a snubbish nose.
If you sneer at it, or scold it, it will scuttle off in shame,
But it purrs and purrs quite proudly if you call it by its name,
And offer it some sandwiches of sealing-wax and soap.

a Use different colours to circle the pairs of words that rhyme.

b Listen for examples of assonance. Write the words on the line below.

____

c Listen for examples of consonance. Write the words on the line below.

____

d Underline any repetition of words or phrases you see.

IMAGINATIVE TEXTS Writing a poem

Write a poem about a platypus or create a mixed-up creature of your own. The features of the platypus are described below.
If you decide to create your own creature, draw it in the box and invent a name for it.

When Europeans who were new to Australia first saw the platypus (*Ornithorhynchus anatinus*), they thought it was a joke. It had a bill like a duck, a body like an otter and a tail like a beaver. It had fur like mammals, but unlike mammals, it had webbed feet and it laid eggs like birds and reptiles. The males also had a poisonous spur on their hind feet.

Plan

1 **Title**

What is the title of your poem? Use the name of your creature as the title.

___

2 **Features of your creature**

List features of your creature and say what the features are like or not like.

a head ___ **d** legs ___
b body ___ **e** neck ___
c tail ___ **f** eyes ___

3 **Habits of your creature**

Make notes about what your creature eats, how it moves and what it likes to do.

___
___

4 **Rhyming words**

List pairs of rhyming words to use in your poem.

___
___

5 **Assonance and Consonance**

Make notes about what your creature eats, how it moves and what it likes to do.

___
___

6 **Refrain**

List words or phrases that you could use in a refrain.

___
___

 TARGETING WRITING SKILLS YR 4 © PASCAL PRESS ISBN 9781925726275

Draft

Now you are ready to write a draft of your poem.

Remember to:

- write the title of the poem first
- write in verse that has a rhythm. Sentences can differ from normal.
- begin each stanza with a capital letter and finish it with a full stop
- write lines of verse with rhymes at the end
- begin each new line with a capital letter
- use examples of assonance and consonance in your poem.

First draft

Write a draft of your poem here.

Feedback

Ask your teacher, classmates or someone at home to suggest what you could do to improve your poem.

Revised draft

Self-evaluation

I wrote ☐ the title on the first line.

I wrote ☐ in verse that has a rhythm.

I began ☐ each stanza with a capital letter and finished it with a full stop.

I began ☐ each new line with a capital letter.

I used ☐ rhyming words at the end of lines.

I included ☐ an example of assonance.

I included ☐ an example of consonance.

PERSUASIVE TEXTS Discussion

The purpose of a discussion is to present different points of view about an issue. It allows the reader to think about different points of view before making an informed decision.

Purpose: The purpose of this discussion is to present different points of view about recycling.

Audience: The intended audience of this discussion is people who are making a decision about the importance of recycling.

Context: Texts like this would be found in newspapers, magazines and online.

A discussion may be accompanied by a photograph or illustration.

A title identifies the topic or issue. It may be in the form of a question.

Is Recycling the Answer to Reducing Waste?

Opening statements introduce the topic and present both sides of the issue.

Recycling saves energy. It saves natural resources. It reduces greenhouse gases. But it can be expensive, and not everything can be recycled.

Subheadings are used to organise the arguments for each point of view. (P)

Recycling saves money

Recycling reduces the need for landfills. Landfills cost money to build and maintain. It costs less to make products from recycled materials. People make money by collecting and selling materials to recycle. Others develop and sell new ways to recycle materials.

A series of paragraphs gives arguments for and against the topic. They provide evidence (E) and explain (E) reasons for holding the point of view.

Recycling costs money

However, it costs to build and operate recycling centres. It costs to collect, transport and process materials to recycle. Recycling costs money. Recyclers do not make money if they cannot sell the recycled material.

A conclusion sums up the discussion and gives a recommendation. It links (L) back to the opening statements.

Towards zero

Recycling is not the whole answer. The best way to reduce waste is to reduce our use of packaging and products. We need products that can be reused, repaired, recycled or composted. That will help us reach a goal of zero waste.

Parts of Speech

Topic-related nouns and noun-groups
- recycling
- greenhouse gases
- landfills
- products
- materials

Present tense
- saves
- reduces
- can
- cost
- develop

Evaluative language
- saves
- reduces
- costs less
- costs
- best
- need

Connectives
- but
- however
- if

Text adapted from *Go Facts: Recycling*, Blake Education.

TARGETING WRITING SKILLS YR 4 © PASCAL PRESS ISBN 9781925726275

Structure of a discussion

PEEL

A discussion presents different points of view about an issue. Often the PEEL structure is used when writing a discussion.

Title

The title identifies the topic or issue to be discussed. Each main word of the title is capitalised.

Circle the title.

Opening statements

The opening statements introduce the topic and present both sides of the topic so that the reader understands the points of view being discussed.

Underline the statements that introduce the topic and the different points of view.

Subheadings

Subheadings are used to organise the arguments for each point of view (P).

Highlight the subheadings which introduce each point of view.

Arguments

A series of arguments provides evidence (E) and explains (E) reasons for the writer's point of view. They link back to the point of view expressed in the heading.

Highlight the words under each subheading that reinforce the point of view.

Conclusion and recommendation

The conclusion and recommendation link back (L) to the opening statements.

Underline the words that link back to the opening statements.

Highlight the recommendation. Do you agree with it? ____________________

Language features of a discussion

Evaluative language

In a discussion, evaluative language is used to make the reader feel about the issue the way the writer does. In the arguments for and against recycling, the writer uses cost as the main evidence. The writer explains the ways in which recycling can cost more or less.

7 **Write the words the writer uses to influence your opinion about the costs involved with recycling.** ____________________

Write the words the writer uses to convince you of the recommendation. ____________________

____

Connectives

Words such as 'but', 'however' and 'if' can be used to connect ideas.

Circle but, however and if in the text.

Writing a discussion

Whenever someone is injured or killed by a shark, many people call for the shark to be hunted and destroyed or for sharks in general to be culled. Others say that the shark should be spared and that all sharks should be protected. Here are some opinions about sharks. Some are based on science while others are based on emotions.

Write a discussion that includes both points of view and presents a recommendation at the conclusion.

Sharks

- ☐ Sharks are important for marine ecosystems.
- ☐ People should be safe from shark attacks when they swim or surf at the beach.
- ☐ Shark attacks are rare and deaths even rarer.
- ☐ Once sharks have tasted human blood, they will hunt more humans.
- ☐ Sharks are scary and dangerous.
- ☐ Sharks attack humans when humans have entered their territory.
- ☐ No one should have to die from a shark attack.
- ☐ It is more important for humans to be safe than to save sharks.
- ☐ Sharks have the right to live in their natural habitat without being hunted and killed.
- ☐ When someone has been attacked, we need to get revenge by finding and killing the shark.
- ☐ More sharks (about 100 million a year) are killed by humans than humans killed by sharks.
- ☐ Many species of sharks are already threatened with extinction.

Plan

1. **Write a title to identify the topic.** ____________________
2. **Some statements are in favour of killing sharks. Some are in favour of protecting sharks.**
   Write **K** in the box if the statement is for killing. Write **P** if the statement is for protecting.
3. **Write an opening statement to introduce both points of view.**
   ____
4. **Write the subheadings that will help organise the arguments for each point of view (P).**
   a ____________________
   b ____________________
5. **Write a concluding statement and recommendation.**
   ____
   ____

TARGETING WRITING SKILLS YR 4 © PASCAL PRESS ISBN 9781925726275

Draft

Now you are ready to write a draft of your discussion.
Remember to:

- write the title first to identify the topic
- write an opening statement to introduce both points of view
- use subheadings to organise the arguments for each point of view (P)
- write a paragraph that presents evidence (E) for and explains (E) each point of view
- write a conclusion that includes a recommendation and links (L) back to the opening statement
- use evaluative language to convince readers of your recommendation
- use capital letters at the beginning of sentences and full stops at the end.

First draft

Write a draft of your discussion here.

Feedback

Ask your teacher, classmates or someone at home to suggest what you could do to improve your discussion.

Revised draft

Self-evaluation

I wrote
- ☐ the title.
- ☐ an opening statement introducing both points of view.
- ☐ paragraphs with evidence and explanations to support the points of view.
- ☐ a conclusion that included a recommendation.

I used
- ☐ subheadings to organise the arguments.
- ☐ evaluative language.
- ☐ capital letters and full stops correctly in sentences.

RECREATING TEXTS Persuasive discussion

The purpose of an exposition is to argue the case either for or against a topic.

Purpose: The purpose of this exposition is to present an argument for or against team sports.

Audience: The intended audience of this exposition is people who are making a decision about the benefits of team sports.

Context: Texts like this would be found in school newsletters, newspapers, magazines and online.

Team Sports

Year 4 students participated in a survey asking their opinion of team sports. These are some of their responses.

The 'up' side of team sports

Kai: "Team sport is great for making friends. You all have something in common."

Emma: "Even when you lose, you still have each other."

Lucas: "Teams always support each other. That makes me feel confident."

Prisha: "You don't have to be good at everything to be useful to the team."

Brooke: "Knowing I made a difference to the team makes me feel good about myself."

The 'down' side of team sports

Billy: "When I'm last to be chosen for a team, I feel embarrassed and ashamed."

Abbey: "People who get too competitive and aggressive spoil the fun."

Advik: "I feel bad if I miss a catch, like I've let down the team."

Mimi: "It's hard if you don't get picked for a game, or you have to sit on the bench for ages."

Eve: "There's too much pressure in team sports. I like to set my own challenges."

Text adapted from Health & Understanding, Blake Education.

Read the students' opinions about team sports. Highlight the most important points for each argument.

Write what you think about team sports and give a reason.

____

____

List some evaluative language you could use to convince readers of your point of view.

____

TARGETING WRITING SKILLS YR 4 © PASCAL PRESS ISBN 9781925726275

✿ Write an exposition stating your opinion of team sports

You have read two sets of opinions, some in favour of team sports and some not. You have also written your own opinion.
Now you will write an exposition to persuade readers to accept your point of view. Include opinions from the survey to strengthen your argument. You may include opposing views, as long as you argue against them. Your exposition should conclude with your recommendation. Do not copy the words from the survey exactly. Express them in your own words.
Remember to:

- write the title to identify the topic
- write opening statements to introduce your point of view (P)
- write short paragraphs to present your arguments with evidence (E) and explanations (E)
- write a concluding statement to sum up your point of view, link back to the opening statement (L) and make a recommendation
- use emotive words and evaluative language to sway the opinions of readers
- use capital letters at the beginning of sentences and full stops at the end.

✿ First draft

Write a draft of your exposition here.

____

____

____

____

____

✿ Feedback

Ask your teacher, classmates or someone at home to suggest what you could do to improve your exposition.

____

✿ Revised draft

____

____

____

____

____

✿ Self-evaluation ✿

I wrote
- ☐ the title to identify the topic.
- ☐ an opening statement to introduce my point of view (P).
- ☐ short paragraphs to provide evidence (E) and explanations (E).
- ☐ a concluding statement to link back (L) and recommendation.

I used
- ☐ emotive words and evaluative language.
- ☐ capital letters and full stops in sentences.

TERM 4

REVIEW

COMPLEX SENTENCES

A **complex sentence** has two or more clauses. It has one **main** or **principal clause** that tells the main idea. It makes sense on its own.

A **subordinate** or **dependent clause** gives more information about the main idea in the principal clause. Subordinate or dependent clauses do not make sense on their own.

Subordinate clauses may be linked to the principal clause by a conjunction or a relative pronoun which is found at the beginning of the subordinate clause. A subordinate clause can occur at the beginning, the end or in the middle of a sentence. When it is in the middle of a sentence, it is called an **embedded clause**.

1 Read these complex sentences. Highlight the principal clause. Underline the subordinate clause. Circle the conjunction or relative pronoun used to link the clauses.

a The children who play interschool sport are wanted on the oval now.
b Many people are afraid of sharks because they have sharp teeth.
c Although it was the middle of winter, we went to the beach every day.
d Our house was renovated while we were away on holidays.
e Unless I finish my homework, I won't be allowed to play my game.
f Since it is the school holidays, I am allowed to stay up late.
g Whenever he comes to visit, my uncle always brings me a present.
h The snake that we saw in the garden is a python.
i Indigenous Australian peoples, who have lived in Australia for tens of thousands of years, managed Country with fire.
j That's a very funny insect that you do not often see.

INFORMATIVE TEXT – EXPLANATION

An explanation explains how things happen or why things are.

(1) Eggs
(2) Tadpole
(3) Back legs appear
(4) Front legs appear
(5) Tail is absorbed
(6) Frog

Use this diagram to write an explanation of a frog's life cycle.

2 Write a title for your explanation. Remember, it is often written as a question.

____

____

3 Write a general statement to introduce your topic.

____

____

4 Write sentences to explain each step of the frog's life cycle.

a ______________________________
b ______________________________
c ______________________________
d ______________________________
e ______________________________
f ______________________________

5 Write a final statement to conclude your explanation.

____

____

 TARGETING WRITING SKILLS YR 4 © PASCAL PRESS ISBN 9781925726275

IMAGINATIVE TEXT – POETRY

The purpose of poetry is to help us understand and appreciate the world around us.

Write a poem about one of the animals pictured.

6 **What is the title of your poem? Use the name of your creature as the title.**

____

7 **List features of your creature and say what the features are like or not like.**

a head ______________ d legs ______________

b body ______________ e neck ______________

c tail ______________ f eyes ______________

8 **List pairs of rhyming words you could use in your poem.**

____

9 **Write a poem that explains what your animal looks like.**

____

____

____

____

PERSUASIVE TEXT – DISCUSSION

The purpose of a discussion is to present different points of view about an issue.

A group of Year 4 children were discussing whether they should be able to have a later bedtime. These are some of the things they thought about: What will I do with the extra time? How will I feel in the morning? Will I want to sleep longer in the morning? Will it make me late for school? Their parents were also discussing the same issues for the children.

10 a List reasons the children might have for staying up later.

____

____

b List reasons the parents might have for children not staying up later.

____

____

11 **Write a discussion that presents both sides of the topic. Write a concluding statement with a recommendation.**

____

____

____

____

____

ANSWERS

Answers are not provided where students are asked to write their own texts.

TERM ONE

Unit 1

Page 2

1 a Q b S c C d E e S

2 Answers will vary. Examples:
- a The children are playing at the beach.
- b Where are the children playing?
- c Look at the children playing at the beach.
- d Watch out!

3 Answers will vary. Examples:
- a The gardener trimmed the hedge with shears.
- b Who won the match on the weekend?
- c Arrest that burglar!
- d That bird looks funny.

Page 3

1
- a I brought my new bag to school. My dad gave it to me for my birthday.
- b The car ran out of petrol. It broke down.
- c The blue whale is the biggest mammal that ever lived. It grows to 30 metres in length.
- d There are eight planets in the solar system. Earth is the third closest to the sun.
- e Frozen water is called ice. It melts when it gets hot.

5 **The Platypus**

The platypus is a monotreme. It is a mammal that lays eggs.
Platypuses lay their eggs in riverbank burrows. The eggs hatch after about 10 days.
Platypuses live on land and in the water. They have thick fur, flat paddle-like tails and webbed front feet.
A platypus uses its bill to find its way underwater and to hunt prey.
When swimming, a platypus closes its nose, eyes and ears. Its bill is good for digging. It also has a special ability. It can pick up electrical signals from insects, worms and frogs. This is called electroreception.

Unit 2

Page 5

1-4 **Canberra Bushfires**

People in Australia live with the threat of bushfires every summer. Even major cities can be damaged by raging fires.

Fire in the capital

It happened on 18 January 2003 in Canberra, the nation's capital. High temperatures and powerful winds combined to produce dangerous firestorms.
By the middle of the afternoon, the sky had turned red. The smoke was so thick that drivers couldn't see without their car headlights.
Everyone thought people's homes would be safe, but they weren't. The fires jumped across firebreaks. They roared into the bushy south-western suburbs. Some suburbs were evacuated.
The government declared a state of emergency.
Firefighting helicopters dropped water bombs on the fires, but strong winds fanned the fires and the firefront kept growing.
Flames stripped the roofs and windows from houses.
By the time the fires were out, four people had lost their lives.
More than 350 homes had been destroyed and another 200 homes had been damaged.

3
- a Canberra 2003
- b thick smoke reduced visibility
- c homes weren't safe
- d firefront kept growing

5 bushfires, raging fires, dangerous firestorms, fires, firebreaks, firefighting helicopters, firefront, flames

6 Answers will vary. Examples:
- a The smoke, from the bushfires, was so thick drivers couldn't see.
- b The fires jumped across firebreaks, barriers built to prevent fires spreading.
- c The government, of Australia, declared a state of emergency.
- d Flames, from the bushfires, stripped the roofs and windows from houses.

Unit 3

Page 6

1-3 **Australian Floods 2022**

more than 20 people died
thousands of people lost homes
businesses ruined
over $2 billion in damages

O one of Australia's worst-ever natural disasters
O flooding in late February, March and April 2022
1 began November 2021 – wettest November on record
2 wet summer – filled the catchments and saturated the ground
3 February – more rain fell in short time since records began in 1800s
C wettest period and worst flooding in Australia's history – caused by combination of La Niña weather system and Southern Annular Mode
5 March – flood situation was declared a national emergency
4 first week in March – southern Qld and northern NSW received a year's rainfall in a week
7 7 April – Sydney got a month's rain in one day
6 by end March, Sydney had already received its annual rainfall
O east coast of Australia flooding from as far north as Maryborough and as far south as Sydney

4 Answers will vary. Example: Australia's Worst-Ever Flood

Unit 4

Page 9

1-4 **A Strange Land**

The land is tough and dry with brown grasses that feel like razors.
Bark peels off trees like skin off a snake. When the wind passes through them it feels like the land comes alive and the trees roar with strange sounds.
A river winds its way through the land and empties into an enormous lake. A scrubby mountain range rises behind it.
There are thousands of flies and biting insects. At times the noise of insects is deafening.
The bush is terrifying one minute and beautiful the next. At certain times of the day, the light makes it look like a beautiful English garden. Other times it appears to be the harshest place on Earth.

3 grasses, trees, river, lake, range, bush, light

4 terrifying, beautiful, beautiful English garden, harshest place on Earth

5 a S b P c M d P e S f M

6 Answers will vary.

Unit 6

Page 13

1-5 **Stop Climate Change Now!**

Our climate is changing. Natural disasters like droughts, floods and fires are occurring more often and cause great destruction.
The only way we can stop climate change is for everyone to help reduce greenhouse gases. Even small changes that you make can help.
Petrol-guzzling cars churn out tonnes of greenhouse gases every year. You must stop using your car every time you go out. You should walk, ride, or use buses and trains. If you must have a car, you should choose a small or electric car.
Even your home makes greenhouse gases. Reduce how much energy you use. It's easy. Use energy-efficient appliances. Turn off appliances when you are not using them. Take shorter showers.
Solar power produces zero greenhouse gases, so you should install solar panels. If everyone used solar power, there would be fewer greenhouse gases.
We must stop climate change now. Everything we do makes a difference.

6
- a Petrol-guzzling cars churn out tons of greenhouse gases every year.
- b Even your home makes greenhouse gases.
- c Solar power produces zero greenhouse gases, so you should install solar panels.

7
- a If you must have a car, you should choose a small or electric car.
- c If everyone used solar power, there would be fewer greenhouse gases.

TARGETING WRITING SKILLS YR 4 © PASCAL PRESS ISBN 9781925726275

8 Answers will vary. Examples:
- a Air conditioners pollute! Turn off your air conditioner. Open a window instead. Fresh air is good for you and the environment.
- b Don't be a polluter! Stop wasting food. When you waste food, you contribute greenhouse gases and climate change.
- c You must reduce your use of plastic bottles and recycle the ones you do use. The plastic bottle you throw away today will still exist in 450 years. What a senseless waste.

Unit 8

Page 16

1 **My Country by Dorothea Mackellar**

The love of field and coppice,
Of green and shaded lanes.
Of ordered woods and gardens
Is running in your veins,
Strong love of grey-blue distance
Brown streams and soft dim skies
I know but cannot share it,
My love is otherwise.
I love a sunburnt country,
A land of sweeping plains,
Of ragged mountain ranges,
Of droughts and flooding rains.
I love her far horizons,
I love her jewel-sea,
Her beauty and her terror –
The wide brown land for me!

2 Answers will vary. Examples:

England:
- a green, grassy fields
- b shady lanes
- c organised gardens

Australia:
- d wide, flat land
- e high rocky mountains
- f beautiful blue sea

3 Answers will vary.

Term 1 Review

Page 18

1 Answers will vary. Examples:
- a (Q) Who kicked the ball into the net?
  (C) Kick the ball into the net at practice today.
  (E) Kick the ball into the net!
- b (Q) What song did the children sing?
  (C) Sing the school song next.
  (E) Sing!

2 A black creature poked out from beneath the rotting logs. Its thin tongue searched for air. The movement caught Kevin's eye. Was it a snake or a lizard? No! It was just an echidna searching for termites.

3 Answers will vary.

Page 19

4 Answers will vary. Examples:
- a sand dunes – piled high like scoops of mango ice cream
- b trees – with branches stretching tall to reach the sky
- c water – muddy water collected in tiny pools shaped like dinosaur footprints
- d grass – dry and broken
- e sky – blue and cloudless

5-10 Answers will vary.

TERM TWO

Unit 9

Page 20

1
- a Synthetic materials include glass and plastic.
- b Materials for clothes need to be soft and lightweight.
- c Materials for buildings need to be hard and strong.
- d Plastic is waterproof, so people make water bottles with it.
- e Most books are made of paper because it is light and flexible.
- f Some books are made of plastic, so babies can play with them in the bath.

2
- S a People use materials to make things.
- F b natural materials from the environment
- S c Scientists research how to change and mix materials.
- S d Synthetic materials are made by people.
- F e materials for buildings
- S f Glass is transparent, so people put it in windows.
- S g Paper is a natural material made from trees.
- F h needs to be hard and tough

Unit 10

Page 23

1-3 & 4b **Odds and Evens are Sweet for Honeybees**

By B. Sweetman

We used to think only we humans could understand odd and even numbers. Now scientists have found that honeybees can learn their odds and evens too. The scientists published their findings in the journal Frontiers in Ecology and Evolution in April 2022.

The scientists put the bees into two groups. They gave one group sugar water with even numbers, and a bitter liquid with odd numbers. They gave the other group sugar water with odd numbers, and the bitter liquid with even numbers. The numbers were shown with shapes like dots or triangles. They were not shown in digits.

The bees quickly learned to choose the number of shapes that would give them the sweet water. They even correctly chose numbers they had not seen before.

This discovery has helped scientists to better understand the ways brains work. Now they have many new questions to find answers to.

3 Answers will vary. Examples:
- a bees recognise odds and evens
- b two groups
- c learn quickly

4 a This discovery has helped scientists to better understand the ways brains work.

5 honeybees, bees

6
- a We used to think only we humans could understand odd and even numbers.
- b People used to think only humans could understand odd and even numbers.

Unit 11

Page 24

1 & 2 **What:** over 30,000 pelicans
Where: Lake Brewster in the Lachlan Valley and Kieeta Lake in the Murrumbidgee Valley, New South Wales
When: early 2022
Why: to breed
Why: the lakes full of water and teeming with fish after a wet summer
Other facts:
- 3 each chick eats up to 1 kilogram of food a day
- 3 chicks and adults require 15–30 tonnes of food (1 tonne = 1000 kilograms)
- 2 rare to have such large numbers
- 2 last time such large numbers of pelicans arrived was after the 2016 floods
- 2 more than twice the average number of pelicans
- 4 not vulnerable or under threat, but numbers declining
- 4 events like this are important for the pelican population
- 5 drones and artificial intelligence (AI) are used to count the pelicans
- 5 joint study by university researchers, conservationists and state officials
- 5 pelicans are banded so researchers can find out more about them

3 Answers will vary. Example: Researchers will study the banded pelicans to find out more about where they go and how they live.

Unit 12

Page 27

1 Title: Bare Feet

2-5 2a B [My four-year-old daughter came to me and said, "Daddy, I'm bored. Can I play outside now?"] 3a
2b M [I was a bit worried about this because we had been renovating our veranda and there were still some leftover nails and small pieces of timber lying around. But it was a lovely day for playing outside, so I agreed. 4
"Ok sweetie," I said. "But make sure you don't have bare feet."] 3b
2c E [Georgie looked carefully at her feet and wiggled her toes 5. Then she looked at me.
"But Daddy," she said. "I don't have bear feet. I have people feet."]

ANSWERS

6 a

b

7 Answers will vary.

Unit 13

Page 28

1-4 **A Fishy Tale**

4a B [Alex had a terrible day fishing on the lake. He sat in the blazing sun all day and didn't catch even one fish.]

4b M [On the way home, he stopped at the fish shop. He ordered four rainbow trout. 3 "Pick out four big ones and throw them at me," he said to the fishmonger.

The fishmonger was confused, but he did what Alex asked. Alex caught the parcel of fish in both hands.]

4c E [When Alex got home, he gave the fish to his mother.

3 "Did you catch them yourself?" she asked.

3 "I sure did," said Alex.]

2 a Alex b fishmonger c Alex's mother

Unit 14

Page 31

1-5 **Stop Wasting Food**

Food wastage produces greenhouse gases which cause climate change. We need to stop wasting food now.

Millions of people do not have enough food. However, almost one third of the food produced is wasted. If we stopped wasting food, there would be enough to feed everyone. It would help save our environment too.

When food is dumped into landfill, it begins to rot. It can take months for it to decompose. Rotting food releases methane which is much stronger than carbon dioxide. If we stopped wasting food, it would be the same as taking millions of cars off the road.

It takes a lot of water and energy to produce food. When food is wasted, the water and energy used to produce it is wasted too. Throwing away one hamburger wastes as much water as having a 90-minute shower.

Most food waste occurs in our own homes. We must purchase our food wisely and stop wasting food now.

6 a Millions of people do not have enough food.
b When food is dumped into landfill, it begins to rot.
c It takes a lot of water and energy to produce food.
d Most food waste occurs in our own homes.

7 a If we stopped wasting food, there would be enough to feed everyone.
b If we stopped wasting food, it would be the same as taking millions of cars off the road.

8 Answers will vary. Example: If we stopped taking long showers, there would be more water and energy for producing food.

9 Answers will vary. Examples:
a Millions of people are dying of starvation because they don't have enough food.
b An enormous amount of water and energy is required to produce your food.
c It takes a very long time for food to decompose. All the while, it is producing methane gas which is harmful to the environment.

Unit 16

Page 34

1-3 **School Lunchtimes Should Be Shorter**

School lunchtimes are too long. They should be shorter.

Children miss out on valuable learning time when they are running around in the playground. There is so much for them to learn. They cannot learn it all when they have such long lunchtimes.

Some people say they need the exercise. I think they really need to exercise their brains. If they walked to school or rode their bikes, they would get more exercise anyway. They don't need to get it at school.

If they have a big breakfast in the morning and big afternoon tea when they get home, they won't need to eat lunch at school. That's just time wasting. Many of them throw their lunch into the bin anyway.

In fact, I don't think children need lunchtimes at school at all. They need more time in the classroom, so they will learn more and be smarter.

4 Answers will vary.

Term 2 Review

Page 36

1 a F at the fish shop
b F dumped into landfill
c S A good comic strip makes me laugh.
d S Food wastage contributes to climate change when rotting food makes methane.
e F not enough playtime

2-7 Answers will vary.

TERM THREE

Unit 17

Page 38

1 a The car wouldn't start, for it had a flat battery.
b We cooked the cake for the right time, yet it wasn't cooked through.
c My big brother can play the guitar, and he can sing at the same time.
d My mother is a teacher, but she doesn't work at my school.
e My book was overdue at the library, so I had to return it.
f We can go to the beach, or we can go to the movies.

2 a I took my umbrella with me, for it looked like rain.
b Gold is an expensive metal, yet it is used in a lot of jewellery.
c Plastic causes pollution in the ocean, so we must dispose of it safely.
d We could watch a movie, or we could go to the beach.
e We could watch a movie in the morning, and we could go to the beach in the afternoon.
f The elephant is the largest land animal, but it is not the largest living animal.

Page 39

3 a Tarantulas are the biggest spiders in the world. They are the scariest spiders in the world. They are not really dangerous to people. Tarantulas are carnivores. They eat insects and other small animals. Tarantulas are nocturnal. They hunt for food at night. Tarantulas have eight eyes. They can't see very well. Tarantulas taste with the hairs on their bodies. They smell with their feet. Many tarantulas live in burrows. Some tarantulas live in trees.

b Tarantulas are the biggest spiders in the world. They are the scariest spiders in the world, yet they are not really dangerous to people. Tarantulas are carnivores, so they eat insects and other small animals. Tarantulas are nocturnal, so they hunt for food at night. Tarantulas have eight eyes, but they can't see very well. Tarantulas taste with the hairs on their bodies, and they smell with their feet. Many tarantulas live in burrows, but some tarantulas live in trees.

Unit 18

Page 41

1-5 **Draw a Spider Dice Game**

Take turns to roll a dice and draw a spider. Draw three spiders to win. Any number can play.

Equipment

- a dice
- a pencil for each player
- a piece of paper for each player

Rules

- Draw the cephalothorax before adding other body parts.
- Draw the abdomen before adding spinnerets.
- All spiders can be in progress, but each spider requires its own rolls of the dice.

What to roll

6 = cephalothorax 4 = legs 2 = pedipalps
5 = abdomen 3 = eyes 1 = spinnerets

How to play

1. Take turns to roll the dice and draw the corresponding body part.
2. Miss a turn if there is nowhere to draw the body part.
3. The first to draw three entire spiders is the winner.

6 draw, take, miss

7 a • a piece of bread • butter • a plate • a knife
b 1 Put a slice of bread on the plate.
2 Use the knife to scrape some butter from the container.
3 Use the knife to spread the butter on the bread.

TARGETING WRITING SKILLS YR 4 © PASCAL PRESS ISBN 9781925726275

Unit 20

Page 45

1 & 6-9

Goats Eat Anything

Not so long ago, Mr and Mrs Kent lived in a cottage in the country. Along one side of the house was a cottage garden, bright with flowers. Lovely smells from the herb garden wafted everywhere and big, red strawberries waited to be picked. Mr and Mrs Kent had to go out to work, so weeds and grass and rubbishy plants, such as fireweed, sprouted madly everywhere.
One day, someone gave Mr and Mrs Kent two goats.
P "I hope they don't scare our grandchildren," said Mrs Kent.
P "Goats eat almost anything," said Mr Kent.
P "Not grandchildren I hope," said Mrs Kent, laughing.
P "No," said Mr Kent. "But I hope they eat fireweed."
P Mrs Kent said, "We'll soon find out."
The next day, when the Kents got home from work, they discovered that the goats not only ate the fireweed, but they ate everything else in the garden too.

2 Mr and Mrs Kent

3 not so long ago, in the country

4 Mr and Mrs Kent's garden was full of weeds.

5 The goats ate the weeds.

10 "Oh no! The goats ate my strawberries," said Mrs Kent.

Unit 22

Page 49

1-6

The Bad Guys

DreamWorks Animation, 2022
Directed by Pierre Perifel
[The Bad Guys is a very funny movie] based on *The Bad Guys* books by Aaron Blabey.
The bad guys are notorious villains. The gang leader is Mr Wolf. Other members are Snake, Piranha, Shark and Tarantula.
The gang plans to steal a valuable award at a fancy gala, but their plan fails, and they are arrested.
To avoid jail, they ask for help to become good guys, but they are pretending. They really want another chance to steal the award. At the end, the gang decides they would rather be bad anyway.
The movie is filled with twists, complications and surprises. It is both hilarious and intriguing from start to finish. Adults and children alike will enjoy *The Bad Guys*.
I give *The Bad Guys* 5 out of 5 stars.
I recommend it for families who like to have a laugh together.

7 a The Bad Guys is a very funny movie.
b It is both hilarious and intriguing from start to finish.
c I recommend it for families who like to have a laugh together.

8 Examples:
a The Bad Guys is an extremely boring movie.
b The movie is completely stupid from start to finish, with extremely uninteresting characters.
c I give this movie one out of five stars and don't recommend it for anyone.

9 Answers will vary. Example: The movie is filled with twists, complications and surprises.

Unit 24

Page 52

1-4

Jump!

It was the summer holidays, and the boys were playing cricket in Owen's backyard. The game was going well, until Nathan hit the ball onto the roof of the garage. He climbed up to get it, but then he couldn't get down.
"Come on," said Nick. "Jump! I dare you."
Nathan wriggled to the edge of the roof and looked down. The path below where Nick and Owen were standing was made of concrete.
"Yeah, come on," said Owen. "Jump. It's not far. I did it last week, and I survived."
"Are you scared?" asked Nick.
"No," said Nathan.
Owen did a pretend yawn. He turned to Nick and said, "He's going to be up there all day. Let's go and watch TV."
"Wait," Nathan said. "Don't go. I'll jump."
Nathan silently counted to ten. Then he closed his eyes and jumped.

5 Answers may vary. Example: Nathan may have broken his leg.

6 Answers may vary. Example: Nathan might not have got hurt and decided that heights and jumping off the roof were fun things to do.

7 Answers may vary. Example: "Don't do it, Nathan!" said Nick. "I was lucky," said Owen. "But it really is dangerous!"

Term 3 Review

Page 54

1 a The bat colony lives near us, and the bats fly over our house every evening.
b Emus can't fly, but they are birds.
c The man said he had a sore leg, yet he walked without a limp.
d We can have pizza for dinner, or we can have fish and chips.
e The children were tired when they got home, for it was a long walk from the playground.
f The ground was very wet after the rain, so the soccer match was cancelled.

2 a The lift was crowded, so we waited for the next lift.
b I couldn't find anything on my desk, for it was very messy.
c It was a very wet day, but they went to the beach anyway.
d The farmer went to the market, and he sold his produce at a stall.
e You could ride your bike to school, or you could catch a bus to school.
f He said he didn't like pizza, yet he ate it anyway.

3 a Snap
b to win all the cards
c a pack of cards
d Answers may vary. Example:
Rules
- Deal out all the cards.
- Players take turns to place a card face up on the pile.
- If two consecutive cards are the same, players yell, "Snap!" The first to yell "Snap!" takes the pile of cards that has been played so far.
- Play continues until one player has won all the cards.

e Answers may vary. Example:
How to play
1 Deal out all the cards.
2 Take turns to place a card face up on the table.
3 Yell, "Snap!" if two consecutive cards are the same.
4 Take the pile of cards if you were the first to yell, "Snap!"
5 Continue playing until one player has won all the cards.

Page 55

4-7 Answers will vary.

TERM FOUR

Unit 25

Page 56

1 a Although Ollie ran fast, he didn't win the race.
b While we were on the bus, we saw a plane take off from the runway.
c Since it was stormy, we had my party inside.
d My favourite books are fantasy stories that have witches and wizards and magic.
e This plumber was the cheapest, therefore we gave him the job.
f If we don't act soon, the climate will continue to change.
g This is my friend whose birthday is today.

Page 57

2 a-e Answers will vary.

3 Our Summer Picnic

One Sunday in summer, our family decided to go for a picnic in the mountains. (After we stopped for morning tea at Grandma's house, we packed the picnic baskets into the car.) (We drove to a place in the mountains that is called Swanfels.) (The picnic ground was once part of the Swanfels School, which was closed in 1986.) (When we arrived at the picnic grounds, I helped my cousins with the picnic baskets.) (After we found a chair for Grandma, we played on the playground equipment.) We had fun on the swings, monkey bars and slippery slide.
Then we went for a walk. (We walked along a track until we came to an old wooden bridge.)
(When we arrived back at the picnic area, we were all very thirsty and hungry.) (Lunch was the best picnic that we ever had.)

ANSWERS

Unit 26

Page 59

1 Title: How Have Indigenous Australian Peoples Managed Country for Tens of Thousands of Years?

2 Statement that introduces the topic: Fire was one of the main tools used by Indigenous Australian peoples to manage Country.

3 Three benefits of using fire to manage Country:
- **a** They used fire to create habitats to attract animals to an area.
- **b** Indigenous Australian peoples knew the best times for lighting fires and made sure that only the underbrush burned.
- **c** The fires also helped useful plants to grow and stopped the spread of plants that weren't useful.

4
- **a** Cause: managing country
- **b** Effect: Indigenous Australian peoples could live sustainably for tens of thousands of years.

5
a	is	**d**	know	**g**	help	**j**	change
b	use	**e**	make	**h**	clear		
c	are	**f**	prevent	**i**	build		

6
- **a** Fire was one of the main tools that Indigenous Australian peoples used to manage Country.
  Fire **is** one of the main tools that Indigenous Australian peoples **use** to manage Country.
- **b** Some Indigenous Australian peoples cleared land to plant crops.
  Some Indigenous Australian peoples **clear** land to plant crops.

Unit 27

Page 60

1 Answers will vary. Example: How do wind turbines work?

2 Answers will vary. Example: Wind turbines use wind to produce energy.

3 Answers will vary. Examples:
- **a** The wind blows.
- **b** The wind turns the blades.
- **c** The blades turn the main shaft.
- **d** The main shaft turns the generator.
- **e** The generator converts mechanical energy into electrical energy.

4 Answers will vary. Examples:
- **a** When the wind blows, it turns the blades.
- **b** When the blades turn, they turn the main shaft.
- **c** The main shaft turns the generator, which converts mechanical energy into electrical energy.

5 Answers will vary. Example: Because the wind doesn't blow all the time, other sources of energy are also required.

6 Answers will vary. Examples:
- **a** kinetic energy – energy caused by movement, for example, of the wind
- **b** mechanical energy – energy of an object moving, for example, a machine
- **c** electrical energy – energy that can be used for powering other things

7 blows, turns, converts, uses

Unit 28

Page 63

1-4

The Triantiwontigongolope
by C. J. Dennis

There's a very funny insect that you do not often spy,
And it isn't quite a spider, and it isn't quite a fly;
It is something like a beetle, and a little like a bee,
But nothing like a woolly grub that climbs upon a tree.
Its name is quite a hard one, but you'll learn it soon, I hope.
So try:
Tri-
Tri-anti-wonti-
Triantiwontigongolope.
But of course you haven't seen it; and I truthfully confess
That I haven't seen it either, and I don't know its address.
For there isn't such an insect, though there really might have been
If the trees and grass were purple, and the sky was bottle green.
It's just a little joke of mine, which you'll forgive, I hope.
Oh, try!
Tri-
Tri-anti-wonti-
Triantiwontigongolope.

5 a & d

It lives on weeds and wattle-gum, and has a funny face;
Its appetite is hearty, and its manners a disgrace.
When first you come upon it, it will give you quite a scare,
But when you look for it again, you find it isn't there.
And unless you call it softly it will stay away and mope.
It trembles if you tickle it or tread upon its toes;
It is not an early riser, but it has a snubbish nose.
If you sneer at it, or scold it, it will scuttle off in shame,
But it purrs and purrs quite proudly if you call it by its name,
And offer it some sandwiches of sealing-wax and soap.

5 b it will give, stay away, trembles tread

c weeds and wattle-gum, funny face, trembles tickle tread toes, sneer scold scuttle shame, purrs purrs proudly, sandwiches sealing-wax soap

Unit 30

Page 67

1-6 & 9

Is Recycling the Answer to Reducing Waste?

Recycling saves energy. It saves natural resources. It reduces greenhouse gases. But it can be expensive, and not everything can be recycled.

Recycling saves money

Recycling reduces the need for landfills. Landfills cost money to build and maintain.
It costs less to make products from recycled materials.
People make money by collecting and selling materials to recycle. Others develop and sell new ways to recycle materials.

Recycling costs money

However, it costs to build and operate recycling centres.
It costs to collect, transport and process materials to recycle.
Recycling costs money. Recyclers do not make money if they cannot sell the recycled material.

Towards zero

Recycling is not the whole answer. The best way to reduce waste is to reduce our use of packaging and products. We need products that can be reused, repaired, recycled or composted. That will help us reach a goal of zero waste.

7 costs, costs, costs

8 best, need, reach a goal

Unit 31

Page 68

1 & 2 Sharks

P Sharks are important for marine ecosystems.
K People should be safe from shark attacks when they swim or surf at the beach.
P Shark attacks are rare and deaths even rarer.
K Once sharks have tasted human blood, they will hunt more humans.
K Sharks are scary and dangerous.
P Sharks attack humans when humans have entered their territory.
K No one should have to die from a shark attack.
K It is more important for humans to be safe than to save sharks.
P Sharks have the right to live in their natural habitat without being hunted and killed.
K When someone has been attacked, we need to get revenge by finding and killing the shark.
P More sharks (about 100 million a year) are killed by humans than humans killed by sharks.
P Many species of sharks are already threatened with extinction.

3 Answers will vary. Example: When shark attacks occur, many people call for the shark to be killed. However, many sharks are already threatened with extinction and far few people are killed by sharks than sharks by people.

4 Answers will vary. Examples:
- **a** a No one should have to die from a shark attack
- **b** b Protect sharks from extinction

TARGETING WRITING SKILLS YR 4 © PASCAL PRESS ISBN 9781925726275

5 Answers will vary. Example: Sharks are not as scary as people think and the number of people killed by sharks is miniscule when compared to the number of sharks killed by people. We must remember that the ocean is their territory and enter with due care to prevent them from going extinct.

Unit 32

Page 70

1 **Team Sports**

Year 4 students participated in a survey asking their opinion of team sports. These are some of their responses.

The 'up' side of team sports

Kai: "Team sport is great for making friends. You all have something in common."

Emma: "Even when you lose, you still have each other."

Lucas: "Teams always support each other. That makes me feel confident."

Prisha: "You don't have to be good at everything to be useful to the team."

Brooke: "Knowing I made a difference to the team makes me feel good about myself."

The 'down' side of team sports

Billy: "When I'm last to be chosen for a team, I feel embarrassed and ashamed."

Abbey: "People who get too competitive and aggressive spoil the fun."

Advik: "I feel bad if I miss a catch, like I've let down the team."

Mimi: "It's hard if you don't get picked for a game, or you have to sit on the bench for ages."

Eve: "There's too much pressure in team sports. I like to set my own challenges."

2 Answers will vary.

3 Answers will vary. Examples: best, most, perfect, fun, wonderful, fantastic, cooperative

Term 4 Review

Page 72

1 a The children who play interschool sport are wanted on the oval now.
  b Many people are afraid of sharks because they have sharp teeth.
  c Although it was the middle of winter, we went to the beach every day.
  d Our house was renovated while we were away on holidays.
  e Unless I finish my homework, I won't be allowed to play my game.
  f Since it is the school holidays, I am allowed to stay up late.
  g Whenever he comes to visit, my uncle always brings me a present.
  h The snake that we saw in the garden is a python.
  i Indigenous Australian peoples, who have lived in Australia for tens of thousands of years, managed Country with fire.
  j That's a very funny insect that you do not often see.

2 Answers may vary. Example: How do Frogs Grow?

3 Answers may vary. Example: Frogs go through many life stages from egg to adult.

4 Answers may vary. Example:
  a Frogs begin life as an egg.
  b Tadpoles hatch out of the eggs.
  c As they grow bigger, tadpoles grow a pair of back legs.
  d Soon after that, their front legs appear.
  e The tadpole's tail is absorbed into the body and disappears as the tadpole becomes a frog.
  f When the frog is an adult, it has no tail.

5 Answers will vary. Example: The adult frog is ready to lay eggs and the life cycle starts all over again.

Page 73

6-11 Answers will vary.

PASCAL
PRESS

Targeting Writing Skills Year 4

ISBN: 9781925726275

Published by Pascal Press
PO Box 250
Glebe NSW 2037
www.pascalpress.com.au
contact@pascalpress.com.au

Design: Janice Bowles
Author: Norah Colvin
Publisher: Lynn Dickinson
Editor: Marie Theodore
Typesetter: Stacey Grainger
Illustrator: Paul Lennon

Printed by Wai Man Book Binding (China) Ltd.